The Alien and Me

This one's for you Larry,

You know what I mean......................

1

CHAPTER ONE

So often my thoughts come from my memories, as I think back to the child I once was, laying on my back in the dew kissed grass, with my knees pointed towards the sky. As I lay there, I was never sure whether I penetrated the night or the night penetrated me, but somehow we would merge and that dark expanse speckled with lights that shone like diamonds helped form who I am today. Calling these dancing lights planets or stars helped me understand that each one of these points had size and mass, but somehow those words made them seem cold and distant. As I would stare into the night skies each individual light seemed to have a life of its own. Some nights these piercing white lights would take on an emotional appearance. They could laugh or cry and how they felt was translated into their twinkle. I, like most children had no concept of time, my minutes would meld together into hours of staring upwards beyond my reach before the silence would be broken by my mother yelling for me to come inside before I caught pneumonia.

As a child I remember thinking that this universe must be a very busy place. All those planets had to be supporting a thriving world, just as earth was. I would literally spend hours at a time wondering who these other beings were. Were they like us, or were they different? Did they use and abuse their world like we did with ours? Or did they care more? What were their animals like? So when I found out, that science said what my eyes saw as never ending life, was nothing but a vast wasteland called space, my child's mind became confused and angry.

One of my first reactions was to question the word "space" itself. For me, I had always understood space to be an empty distance between two points. Anyone looking into the nights skies would be hard put, to see it as emptiness. So right from the very beginning my faith in science was observed with cautious restraint. But as time passes and we grow older, life seems to lose some of its magic on us. We allow ourselves to conform to the conditioning of authority. We grow weary trying to maintain our innocence in the onslaught or authoritative condemnation. Our world has become ignorant to the honouring of the rights of the individual.

Maintaining my own personal opinions was starting to become part of my list of personal extinctions. But in my mind I could never quite conform to popular thought. Part of that is the rebel in me and the other part is my own personal interpretation of logic. Life cannot be experienced through a mathematical equation, at least not for me, only the process of feeling can sculpt a state of reality.

Understanding this at a relatively young age set the scene for the kind of life that some would call bizarre. But the word "normal" can only be used in a relative context anyway. So something that many others would call a burden became a blessing in my life, and that blessing was my inability to see the world and its actions through only my physical eyes. There was a sense or perception of a world within a world. All that the eyes could not see, could still be perceived by what felt like a sensory panel that existed in a tubular form which surrounded the body. That tubular form is what most would know as the energy field. An expansive space that is filled with highly charged electrical reactors. They will react to anything within their reach that also has an energy field. I could feel movement that I could not touch, experience sounds that I could not hear, and react to an emotion that there seemed to be no physical evidence of. Life was a multi-level experience. The visual and the non-visual melded into one swirling sea of experience. My brain learned to interpret waves of energy that other people did not notice into delicate detailed pictures or thoughts or beings that would in turn be stored in my mind as knowledge or wisdom.

This at a very young age became my world. I have spoken to so many people throughout my life who wish they saw the world as I do. However as with all gifts or abilities that can make you special, they can also set you apart as well. The greatest disease in the world is that of ignorance. In general our curiosity is nipped in the bud when we are a child and the wonder and awe at the world around us is replaced with someone else's fear. Fear of that which is not known.. We replace acceptance with scepticism and hope quickly becomes despair.

4

However, my world was not like this. Sure it had its problems but I was unable to share in the state of despair that so many deemed a normal part of life. In all people I can see a light. That light is love. Love is the passion that has been forgotten on this planet. Love is the message that is quietly being reawakened within us now. One of the truest statements ever made was " You may not get what you want, but you always get what you need." I don't know who said it but I'm sure they must have led a most interesting life to come to that reasoning. This is the statement in the story of my life. You may find it outlandish,or bizarre or perhaps even unbelievable. This is a story of hope and love. Sometimes these gifts come in strange forms and it is up to us to define the truth of those forms beyond our fears.

Who is to say where life really starts. So many of us like to believe, we can categorize the beginning of life as we know it to be, at the present point. My truth is that there is no beginning point to life. Even before the point of conception it took a thought or an action between two people to create the most profound events in our existence. One that the majority of us don't even remember. It would be much more accurate for us to measure our life cycle as a sequence of events instead of chronological time. My life can be compared to looking through a photo album. Each individual picture is a moment frozen in time. Each moment has its own significance, and its own memory. However if you took each picture and laid them out in the proper sequence, they could tell the story of how I came to be here this very minute on this very day in time. Every individual who saw the groupings of photos would personalize it to their own experience and therefore each would see something different. This book gives my version of life and the events in time as they relate not only to me personally, but also on a Universal level. It takes all of us, living life individually to create a Universal event. I know there are many people besides myself that have lived a life similar to mine. I hope my story will strike a few chords and allow people to understand that silence is no longer the answer. It is only when we come together and share our experiences that we will find truth. And the truth is what will take us beyond our fears. And beyond our fears lies freedom. So for me, this book is my freedom, because it is my truth.

Reality as we have understood it is about to take a drastic change. All of us are currently in varying states of preparation. We are carrying and anchoring in different levels of higher vibrations that earth needs to make this shift. Our level of self awareness and acceptance will define our vibrational rate and our ability to go through this transition with ease. To allow ourselves to grow we must go through experiences to recreate our reality based on our capability for discernment. We have the power in our hands and our hearts to make our future whatever we choose. Choice can be your punishment or your blessing depending on your viewpoint.

But all of life is based on choice whether we realize that or not. Choice controls the events in our lives, and we are responsible for the choices we make. Making conscious choices is the key to relieving ourselves of the burden of fear of control by outside forces. As a very young child I held a fascination for the sequence of events that would follow a choice that was made. I can remember sitting and imagining what would happen if I chose to go in this direction or that. My imagination would create every event, every twist and turn in time until my thoughts took me to the outcome of my choice. At that time I would snap back into the present moment and marvel in amazement at the amount of occurrences that came from one small choice.

And so my life fell into a pattern of knowing an outcome of any particular situation based on a decision I was about to make. Some people would say that was putting the cart before the horse, that this took the mystery or excitement out of life. But for me this was only logical . Why would you make a decision that would take you somewhere you didn't want to be. This process. helped me to fine tune my intuition. It helped me learn that we are not victims in life, but the creators of it.

By following my knowing I began to trust that no matter how illogical a decision was, the sequence of events that followed would take me where I needed to be. Being a child that was fascinated with the world around me and knowing that we individually created our world , it left me to be categorized as strange or unusual by the people that were familiar to me. And so started my journey. My journey was simply to find a state of acceptance from other people and for myself. It doesn't take a child's mind very long to believe something is wrong with them if they are told often enough. In an attempt to become normal I withdrew into myself. I learned early on not to speak of my thoughts, that usually brought some kind of condemnation. I would be OK as long as I stayed quiet. Introverted. became a label that I became all to familiar with. I didn't know what that word meant at the time, but I knew it was not who I was. By withdrawing into myself I found doorways that I hadn't known before. Doorways that when opened, allowed me to go through to the worlds on the other side. However, the other side that I came to know wasn't the same as the world I had come from. This other side was bright and beautiful and filled with many magical beings that didn't seem to exist in the world of adults. So I came to know a world between worlds. Between the waking and dream state. A space where there was no judgement. This spot was the only place I felt totally accepted and completely loved. I knew it was a place that all people could go if only they allowed themselves. There were times, when I was in this alternate space that I would glimpse people I knew as they passed through, like ghostly images.

The images I remember of this place were created of beautiful vibrant colours. There were sounds unlike any I had ever heard. Totally pure and powerful but they didn't hurt your ears. Each tone could penetrate your body, and as it did it would seem to make you tingle with a new vibration. But the image that permanently etched itself in my mind is that of the beings that seemed to come and go on beams of light that gracefully crossed the sky. Beings of all shape and size. Some looked human like, others would change shape as they moved. Still others seemed to be pure energy with no definable features. As I was able to hold my focus in this place for longer periods of time, the beings started communicating with me. some would tell me of their world and others would tell me of the earth and my own life. Even though my logical mind couldn't make sense of this process I was not frightened. Something in the way they spoke to me made me feel loved, comforted and protected. Each one of those beings seemed so familiar to me even though I had never seen them in my world. Through my interaction in this space I came to know that what I had thought of as life was not all there was. I wasn't sure how everything tied together, but I did know one could not exist without the other. The beings had told me this and told me that earth was the key.

At that point I didn't understand this either. I only knew somehow that earth was a deciding factor in the lives of these beings. I had been informed that I was being watched over and had also been told that someday I would tell my story. I was different for a reason. I shouldn't let it bother me because when the time was right I would understand. This all felt very comfortable for me . Finally someone was saying it was O.K. to be different, maybe even beneficial in the end. I liked to feel that someday maybe I might be able to make a difference in this world. So I began to treasure my uniqueness, instead of fight it. But at the same time, I knew, for the sake of my sanity that I must play the games the people around me required me to play, so that they could relax and stop looking at me with fear in their eyes. Time went to work doing its job as efficiently as ever and I started growing up. Ageing set in as my body matured from a child to a young adult. Being different did not leave me immune from the confusion of being a teenager, or the heart break after the ending of my first romance. On the outside things with me appeared to be pretty normal, but on the inside I felt as though I was split in two.

Societies illusion was my deception. I saw man's moralities and his laws and was never quite able to accept them as my own. As I aged I watched society do everything it could do to over complicate and delude itself into believing in its own reality and therefore its own duality. It was beyond my comprehension how or why people seemed to crave pain and suffering. Whether it was self imposed or imposed upon someone else, people couldn't get enough anguish. Oh sure it may have come in the guise of action adventure films or even heroism, but when it came down to it, fear was the basis for all reactions in anger, it fed the population the adrenaline rush they couldn't create in their own lives. I had come from a lifetime of pain and I wanted no more of it. So without consciously knowing it I started to search for love. This search went through the normal process of hiding in relationships and friendships even sordid affairs had a hint of love in them, but nothing offered me even a tiny glimmer of what I had felt as a child in that place I call the ozone. A space where all time can be accessed by all those who are willing to stop fanning their veils of illusion and see the part of themselves that their logical minds would deny.

8

Chapter Two

So this book is a book about Alien experiences with humans as much as it is about human experiences with Aliens. I am no different than anyone else when it comes to my fears . I am not sure that I had believed all Aliens were frightfully intimidating, but my fear was, that they were. Perhaps too much conditioning by television or just part of human nature, I don't know. However, before my experiences the safest place for my mind to keep an Alien was in the lights that travelled across the sky at a speed that was beyond my comprehension. So for me, as for others, any of the encounters I had with them as a child had been veiled from me until I could deal with what had happened Looking back now, I can see much of my life has occurred in a pattern that would be considered preparation for my meeting with other worldly beings. These occurrences however, didn't start happening in fast forward until just a few years ago. I lived in a very small second floor apartment. The building was old and run down but it was home for the time being. I had just gone through a separation after a five year relationship and was attempting to start a new life. As is usual in this type of scenario I would spend a lot of time by myself thinking. We are ruthless being's when it comes to self punishment. We attempt to drive ourselves crazy by rehashing over and over again the mistakes we think we made and how we would do it differently if we only had the chance. All the typical thoughts were going through my mind. The self doubt and wondering if I was wrong or maybe he just didn't love me any more.

It was a very warm summer night and the apartment had a balcony that went right around the building. So feeling a little claustrophobic I grabbed my coffee and a chair and moved out onto the balcony. It was a beautiful night. The sun had just gone down in the west. The sky was that incredibly beautiful azure blue it gets as you head into twilight. It was still light enough that only a few of the brightest stars in the sky were revealing themselves. As I sat and put my feet up on the rails of the balcony I leaned back into the perfect rocking position, I remember thinking. "This must be what heaven is like at night." For a few moments I visited the world of peace and the perfection of a perfectly painted canvas. Even though you could hear the hum of a town retreating under the blanket of darkness, silence seemed the only sound that touched my ears. It was definitely a moment beyond others in time. Then my peaceful mesmerism was broken by a shadow that crossed the right corner of my eye.

My first assumption was that the mosquitoes were starting to make their presence known. Where I live, they are more than profuse in the summer. I lengthened my neck and put my head back and prepared to swat to kill whatever might crave my blood. However I did not see a cloud of pesky skin piercing bugs, I saw five dancing lights in the sky. I kind of blinked my eyes and shook my head at the same time. For some time my logical mind was having a problem assessing what my eyes saw. The sudden disorientation I felt at shaking my head caused my to lose my balance and I went backwards in my chair. The fall seemed to turn itself into one graceful movement however and I immediately returned to my feet. As my gaze returned to the sky I could not rationalize what I saw. The lights were crossing space at a phenomenal rate of speed in what seemed to be a random pattern.

There was no way this could be a shooting star, satellite or even a meteorite shower. I had never seen a meteor that went in one direction only so far and then turned and went in the other direction. As I watched this magical performance I remember feeling these lights were joyful, possibly celebrating something. I am really not to sure how long I watched this process but it was at least ten minutes, and then as quickly as they came they shot off into the east and were gone. It took me a few minutes to shake off the shock of what I had just seen. I can honestly say that Aliens never crossed my mind as I watched the lights. I was too caught up in the beauty of what was happening to wonder who or what was orchestrating it. It was only later when I got on the phone to call my friends, announcing what I had just witnessed, that the sarcastic response returned to me as "Oh, what are you saying, you just saw a UFO?"

Then and only then did it start to register in my mind that this was exactly what had happened. Because of the comments that were made by my so called friends and perhaps to a great extent my own denial, I was quick to chalk the experience up as one that should be kept silent and placed in the ultimate record keeper, my mind.

Although I was not consciously aware of it, that night was the kick off point for my life to change beyond all recognition

One of the advantages I feel exists in my life is the fact the I generally accept the abnormal as normal and question it later. This event was no exception. After the immediate adrenaline rush had calmed down, I went to bed as I usually did without giving it another thought. But as days passed I found myself trying to analyze what I had seen. I watched the television for reports of anything strange or unusual having happened that night. I checked with the weather bureau only to find out what I already knew, that it had been a perfectly clear night. It's not that I was in a state of denial so much as I had the need to satisfy my left brain with a logical answer to the questionable circumstance my eyes had perceived. But no matter how hard I tried to find a reasonable answer nothing came close to offering me what I required. So as all good humans do, I filed the unanswerable into its own little category and placed it neatly away in my brain for future reference. I can't really say this was a state of denial only procrastination.

The one thing I found to be different in my life after seeing the lights was how often I watched the night skies. For the rest of that summer, every time the sky was clear I would look up for awhile and wait, I would wait until I got tired or the mosquitoes drove me inside, but usually if I waited long enough I would see one or more lights manoeuvre themselves in erratic patterns across the surface of the Milky Way and then out of sight. A rational reason I never found but I did discover a growing belief that, we are not alone, and in fact, interplanetary traffic seemed kind of heavy at times. However the autumn of that year brought an ending to the prolific sightings I had observed. For some reason they just seemed to up and disappear.

To this very day I have never seen as many as often as I did that year. But those sightings seemed to plant a seed in me. It was very soon after this that I started to dream of seeing lights in the sky. In my dreams the lights were starting to come closer and closer to the point where I started seeing faint outlines of ships. Then the dreams would start refining the details of the ships and I could make out symbols or writing on the sides. And then one night as I was dreaming of a ship I suddenly heard a voice speak to me and then I was aboard the ship. I travelled through space at a speed I could not comprehend to a destiny I had no knowledge of. I could not see who was talking to me because my vision seemed blocked on the sides so that I could only see forward. I remember being told not to worry, that I was all right. I was also told that I was a part of all this, and I very clearly remember being asked if I would help. I said yes even though I didn't consciously know how or what I was saying yes too.

After agreeing I woke up in my own bed in my own apartment. Even though nothing seemed disturbed or unusual, for as much as I told myself that it was only a dream, I could not get myself to believe it. There was something far too real about all of it. Generally, in my dreams I will dream in colour but my dream state doesn't usually involve all five senses. I can honestly say I could hear, see, smell, touch and taste everything in this dream. The one thing that really stood out in my memory was the smell aboard that ship. If you pay attention to your nose here on earth, you'll find a variety of smells. Whether you are at home or out of doors in the forest. As you move around or shift the position of your head, your nose will perceive the quality of the air in a slightly different manner. This could occur with a slightly different air temperature or moving from the bathroom to the kitchen and smelling different aromas. But no matter what, the air is always changing. Aboard this ship the air seemed fresh and clean there was no air movement. I have never experienced this in a dream before. I can remember smelling the stench of death or the scent of apple blossoms in spring, but never absolute stagnation.

Being consciously aware of this was nothing new to me. I have always looked forward to my dreams. As a matter of fact there have been more nights than I care to recall that because of the lack of dreaming I got bored and woke up usually getting out of bed to have a coffee. Dreaming has always played an important role in my life even as a child. Sometimes my life got a little confusing before I really came to accept that reality in the dream time is different than physical reality. There were many times as a child that I would dream of an occurrence in vivid detail only to have that same event act itself out before my eyes within days of the dream. This little ability I had tended to spook the people around me to a great extent. It doesn't take long for a child to clam up about their thoughts, once they realize they are not welcomed by the adults around them.

"It was only a dream, or that's not real," became two very common phrases in my life. And although I never forgot about my abilities, I did manage to shut them down to be all but non-existent. It wasn't until I was in my early twenties that I started to probe my own mind, once again finding doorways that weren't entirely locked but also weren't that easy to open. What had been an entirely natural process for me once, now made me feel foreign. Someone separate and different. In most cases people saw me as someone to be wary of. People fear that which they don't understand. It was also around this time that a chain of circumstances was set off that would bring about an awakening of my abilities through communication with those that have passed over. Life changes in an instant, and over night I found myself involved in a murder case and the deceased people were communicating with me. I was given intimate details of how the murders had occurred and who was guilty. I had a hard time coping at first. There was just too much information too fast.

I was experiencing so much all of a sudden that I was in a state of chaos. Not only was I unable to control my own life but the people around me didn't know how to handle what was going on. There were many times I sat and wondered, if I scheduled that awakening in that way or if I had help in the construction of that intense time period. So many doors opened up to me in such a short period of time that I needed to shut down for awhile. I was experiencing so much of what people would call non reality that my head was spinning. There was no logical way to explain energy beings. I felt so imposed upon by all this newness that I just wanted it to stop. That attraction, repulsion state set in, where I became totally involved in other dimensional contact, or I completely ignored it. The only problem was that for as much as I tried to deny it at times, I also knew it was part of who I was becoming.

So for more than a year I bounced back and forth between obsession and ignorance. There was no one to formally teach me, or even to guide me in my thoughts with answers for my many questions. I didn't know what was normal in my experience. Everything I learned was by trial and error. But then I met a woman by the name of Marilyn. This woman changed my life. To this day I cannot tell you what it was in exact detail that she did to me or for me, but she allowed me to open up to a whole new level of experience.

Marilyn worked with accessing negative core belief systems, changing them to a positive, and therefore changing a persons life through their cellular memory. Well this process moved through me like some kind of superconductor. Within one month my life totally changed I became separated from my current relationship, moved into a nice little cottage by myself, and that is where I became totally absorbed by the idea that Aliens were coming to get me. I can remember laying in bed at nights not being able to sleep because I had to keep watching for the Aliens. I had myself completely convinced that if I fell asleep they would get me, so I started falling into a pattern of sleeping maybe 2 or 3 hours a night. I would sleep with the lights on and sometimes even a knife under my pillow. What I thought I would accomplish with the knife, I'm not really sure, it just made me feel safer. I could not get over my feeling of paranoia around these images I had seen of Aliens with big black eyes. I didn't know why these Aliens in particular held me as an emotional hostage but my fear was, i would find out.

This was something I didn't feel I could discuss with people either. Most people around me already thought I was crazy, or a witch or something. This absolute fear of Aliens would probably get me put in the nut house if it was to get out. So I allowed time to go on, trying to wish my fear away. That triggered a lot of memories in me. One of the things I kept thinking about for some reason during this time was something that my mother had told me I did when I was a child. As the story goes, the old version of the Outer Limits used to come on television with its opening segment, in that segment there would be a human eyeball that appeared, an up close shot of an eyeball. Every time I saw that eye I would run and hide and they would have to coax me out from my hiding place. Why would a little child under the age of 4 be so terrified of eyes? Was it the human eye or was it just the fact that the eye seemed to be watching me? What was it about eyes? As an adult eyes fascinated me. They are one of my favourite parts of the body.

I suppose in some ways I will never be able to explain this to my satisfaction. However I have always felt that it had something to do with the fear I felt around Aliens. In so many ways I knew that my life was about to change forever. Nothing was the same anymore, anyway. I had gone through such a transformation in the last few months of my life, that, the life I had come to know obliterated the one that had existed, At this point I felt I was only in the world and not of it. I have never liked the feeling of being afraid and I have always believed that the only way to eliminate a fear is to face it. Dealing with my fear of Aliens was the same as dealing with any other fear, live with it or face it.

So in an attempt to cure myself of this disabling emotion, I decided to open some doors. In my mind I sent out a beacon of thought waves. Within this beacon was a request, all I wanted was to be released from the fear. To do this I knew that I must know the truth. Was there really any such thing as Aliens? The one thing I learned was that as much as I said I believed in them, when I really thought about it I was never really sure that they existed The logical mind is a very powerful thing. It is very easy to convince yourself that you have an over active imagination so that you can feel safe. Well for me, safe just didn't cut it anymore. Needing to know where the fears came from became one of the most powerful motivators in my life. So as soon as I made the decision that no matter what, I was going to find out about my fears, I could feel a shift in my life. In some ways nothing seemed to matter anymore. My job became irrelevant, having a social life was put on the back burner, and I even noticed a lack of desire in my life, at least desire for anything but the truth. It was then that I decided to take a course that would give me some of the truth that I desired so much.

It was late August as the calendar measures time. My friend Marilyn was co-teaching with another lady from the US. Supposedly the course material was on accessing core belief systems and becoming a facilitator of them. I am not sure what came over me at this point, but all I new was that I had to take this course. There was much to do to get ready for this, I had io shift my work schedule, arrange for someone to take care of my house, find a tent because I intended to sleep outside and just do the general packing. But everything fell into place almost too smoothly, and before I knew it I was starting another sequence of life changing events that would take me to a new level of how I perceive my reality.

15

Chapter Three

I have always tried to live my life as simply as possible. However, sometimes, what I try to do and what I actually do, are two totally different things. I think sometimes I have a deep seated fear of boredom or at least things being too normal. So through trial and error, I found that when I followed my instincts I would at least be true to myself, and usually find some excitement where there may have been none before. So this course that I was taking was true to form for me. I went into this education with a completely open mind and heart. I knew that something was about to change in my life. It has long been my belief that the living of life comes from the participation in it, or at least being present in experiencing it. For me this course was about going through the experience of being completely present in the experience of life. Now that may be a strange statement, as you think you are always present in your own experiences, but truthfully we tend to dissociate in our everyday lives and therefore shut down our ability to feel on all levels. I knew this course would be intense, it dealt with all levels of our being and how we hide emotionally charged events in our subconscious.. I am the classic case of one who tends to dissociate. It was a survival mechanism for me as a child, growing up in an abusive family. So this course would definitely force me to experience all levels of my being.

I hadn't been in school for many years so staying in class all day was a challenge. Learning, focusing concentrating, they all took their toll and at the end of the day everyone was totally exhausted. It was also years since I had spent any length of time in a tent on the ground. But during lunch break and after classes I managed to get my tent set up and build myself a suitably comfortable bed, have dinner and then retire to my outside accommodations. Strangely enough I was the only person who chose a position in the middle of the field a good distance from the house where most people were staying. There was one other person who was in a tent but they were not within sight of where I was.

At night the stars literally took my breath away. It was late August and it was unusually cold out for this time of year. I was very thankful a friend had loaned me two down sleeping bags, otherwise I probably would have frozen to death. That first night I fell asleep very quickly because I was so tired. My sleep was very sound, which is not the norm for me. I am one of those people who wakes up if a mouse runs across the floor. My sister once said that I sleep so lightly that I would wake up if someone was to drop a feather. So when I suddenly found myself awake at the crack of dawn without having woken through the night I found myself becoming suspicious at having a good nights sleep. However there was no time to indulge in paranoia, so I simply got up and prepared for another day of classes.

Classes were going well, but there was so much to learn. There was very little time to ourselves and so most of us were learning what it means to live in community. It is more difficult than you might expect it would be. So with tensions running somewhat high with new people in new situations I followed my usual pattern of trying to dissociate. But the minute I would start to distract myself from my reality, I would start seeing things. The things that I was seeing were like other beings in the room. Sometimes they would stand behind people and beam them with light, or they would touch them. If I watched carefully I could see the people react to being touched by these unearthly creatures. There were more than a few times I would just sit there and stare, shaking my head at what I was seeing. The thought crossed my mind to wonder what was actually being put in the health food that we were eating.

My logical mind was in total denial that anything I was seeing was real, so I didn't say much at first, I just sat back and waited to hear if anyone else was seeing the same thing as I was. But over the next day or two, no one really said anything in specific about what they were or were not seeing. So I decided to talk to Marilyn about what I was seeing. After all I didn't want to be going crazy and not know it. I felt almost a little embarrassed telling someone else what I was seeing. I mean think of how it must have sounded. But Marilyn took it all in stride. She explained to me that these beings were very real and they were there assisting people through their transition. They, for the most part were supporting everyone's bodies from going into overload by constantly rerunning their energies. The other major role they were playing was just spreading a lot of love around so that we could all feel a little more secure. It felt very good to be validated but it also felt very strange to be able to see these beings that actually exist in another dimension but can interact with us in our dimension. To tell the truth, it almost felt a little intrusive. I mean who invited them anyway, what right do they have to be here? Then I realized, that was my fear revealing itself again.

So once again I retired to my tent and tried to think about these other beings and my unexplained fear, but I was not able to stay awake long enough to be angry or afraid, or anything else for that matter. Dreamland called and obediently I went. When I awoke in the morning, once again I was startled by the soundness of my sleep. It was almost bothering me that I was sleeping so comfortably. Suspicion has always been a part of my nature, so anything I couldn't explain unnerved me. But I followed my regular morning routine and got ready for classes.

Classes were starting to get even more intense now, as we finished with the physiology of the human body and ventured into the emotional realm where most of us live. Going within and facing your own demons is the most difficult thing any one person can ever do. I was just starting to deal with the intensity of my own emotions, when I realized there was a storm rolling in over the hills and I had to make sure that my tent was as leak proof as possible. Offers were put out to me to stay in the house if I needed to, but I was determined to stay in my own private space, in my tent.

As I went to bed that night the lightening display was absolutely incredible. I hadn't experienced anything that powerful for a long time. Going through a thunderstorm in a tent is an occurrence that has to be lived through to be appreciated The electricity in the air, the vibration as it moves through your body when lightening strikes the ground. Even the power of the storm could not keep me awake and I found myself falling asleep. The rhythm of the rain felt like a comfortable old blanket wrapping me in a state of silent bliss. My bliss however was less than gracefully interrupted when I awoke with a sudden start to the sound of a heavy downfall of rain and an even heavier drip, drip, drip in my tent. Now what was I going to do? I was out here in the pouring rain and I was far to tired and stubborn to go inside where it was dry. As quickly as I could I moved everything from the immediate area of the leak and tried to find a towel or something to catch the falling water. I sat there worrying for awhile about what I was going to do. Maybe I would drown and someone would come looking for me in the morning and find me dead? The thoughts that ran through my mind got pretty crazy. My imagination took over and it was all too easy to make a mountain out of a mole hill.

So sitting in my own little dripping haven I proceeded to make even the most outlandish possibility become a reality in my own mind. Letting my imagination take over to the point where I wasn't sure if I was awake or asleep and what state I was existing in. I think I was just enjoying feeling sorry for myself at the time, then all of a sudden the strangest of feeling came over me, it was almost electrical in nature but somehow warm and loving at the same time. I literally had to stop and check to see what was going on in the tent to make sure that I had not fallen asleep again, however I was wide awake. There seemed to be a blue light in the tent that was emanating from within the tent itself. Within seconds I could clearly hear a voice in my head, this voice was saying " Dome the tent, stop the leak" All I could think was, sure I could dome the tent if I had a tarp. But I didn't have a tarp. As soon as that thought stopped the voice was in my head again in a clear firm tone " Use energy to cover the tent create a shield. Do what you know you must do."

I didn't know what the voice meant, but I did feel it should be possible to create an energy shield and have it umbrella the tent so that the leaks would stop. At this point I felt that I had nothing to lose in the attempt. So I proceeded to centre myself and imagine what an energy umbrella would look like as it covered the tent. I tried to create it as real as possible, to be able to see it, feel it and hear the rain hitting it instead of the tent After a few seconds, I thought I could hear the rain hitting the tent differently. I shifted my focus, and as I did that I realized that the constant dripping of the rain coming into the tent had stopped. I really did not believe what was happening. But the proof was right there. Whatever I had done had worked and the rain was no longer entering the tent. Even though I was used to a somewhat abnormal life this was too much, even for me.

Whether it was the energetic exertion from what I just had created or just plain simple brain overload I don't know, but I was suddenly completely overwhelmed with the need to sleep. I think at that point I was asleep before I even put my head down. I really don't know how long I had been asleep, but suddenly once again I was awake. This time was very different though, now there was someone in the tent with me. I went to grab my flashlight when I realized that I could already see. The light was dim but I could see very clearly that the person in my tent was a male. I could not see where the blue light that lit up the tent was coming from. The man who sat calmly before me looked straight into my eyes waiting for me to say something that would acknowledge his presence. But for the moment I was dumbfounded. All I could do was stare at this stranger. Something inside me said he wasn't real. My physical senses said this guy was flesh and blood but my instincts said there was something too perfect about him. Even though he appeared to be physical there was a slight fog surrounding him. The blue light that filled the tent was even more intense around his body. Instead of asking who this guy was, I found myself wondering what he was.

After a few moments I was compelled to speak but my vocal chords did not seem to be working. I was thinking that I should be able to speak, there was nothing stopping me, I was thinking of what I would say to him, when I heard him offer his response to my thoughts. He said he was from a distant place in the galaxy, some called it the Pleiades, although it really had no name. The place he was from was not as much a planet as a dimension. He was here at the course with others of his kind, helping us all shift our energies.

My next thought was to wonder what he was doing visiting me. He said that I was having a lot of fears around Aliens, and he had come to help me see what so-called Aliens really were. He also told me that much experience was coming to me and his visit was a gift to me so that I could understand the way things are to the fullest capacity. He also said it was time for me to go beyond human, to go beyond third dimensional reality, and that I must understand what it is like to feel myself expand beyond physical earth bound reality.

At this point I think all I wanted to do was to get out of that tent and run for the house screaming, that this was some kind of practical joke. But I had also forgotten that he knew my thoughts, and his response to that was, I knew the truth and if I looked inside I would feel who he was. At that second I was suddenly transported through time and space and I seemed to be floating in a place that I could not determine as anything. The man who had been in my tent had joined me. but now he looked much more solid somehow, he motioned for me to look ahead As I did an image of myself appeared, then slowly a coloured line appeared to be coming out from my body. At the end of that line there was another image of another being that looked similar to me but different. Then I was shown where this other being existed and the life they were living. This sequence kept repeating itself at an ever increasing rate of speed until at last it was done. The amount of lives I had seen were too numerous to count. But the most incredible thing happened after this, I could literally feel all of these other lives and how they were a part of me. I was not just human, I was Alien, and all the other forms of life that I had witnessed as well. I didn't know how this was possible but I could feel it to be true.

Then this man that was standing beside me simply said, "You are all that is". And with that we were back in my tent in the eerie blue light that seemed to emanate from nowhere. I suddenly felt as though I didn't want to be on earth anymore, I wanted to return to this place I had just been, earth wasn't my home. What was I doing here? I didn't belong here. I was overcome with emotion, I wanted to go home. The man moved towards me and offered me his hand As I placed my hand in his, a wave of incredible energy moved through me. I would have sworn that my body actually rocked from the force of the movement.

This wave was a pure form of emotional energy. I found myself looking at this being, this man, with complete unquestioning love. Who he was no longer mattered, that he existed did. He then proceeded to ask me if I desired to experience what pure love was and how it could be attained with another human. Its a good thing I didn't have to move my lips because I don't think I could have, my decision was answered with the single thought, yes. What happened then cannot honestly be described by words. This other worldly visitor took me to a place I had never been before with any other being. He showed me that it was possible to completely merge with another human being in a place that goes to and beyond love. I can only describe this feeling as every single cell in my body could feel every single cell in his body and then expanded to the universe itself. This universe that we call home is not really an angry place nor is it evil, it is a simple place that is based in love, all we have to do is to allow ourselves to feel it as it offers itself to us.

When my beautiful experience was over I could feel nothing but love. The man beside me turned to me and said "Always remember this feeling for this is the real world we all live in. This is yours to share and you will know when the time is right. I am with you always." And with that he was gone. I couldn't feel sad that he was gone because I knew he really wasn't. He would always be with me as he said he would and if I ever needed him I knew I had but to call. So with a dry tent and a smile on my face I placed my head on my pillow closed my eyes and went into a place of peace. In the morning I awoke and faced the decision of telling my class mates what had happened or not. I decided that somehow at that point I wasn't really ready to say anything to these people I was sharing life with at the moment. For me, what had happened was very personal and very intimate and to tell the truth I wasn't sure if anyone would believe me. I thought more than likely everyone would think I was getting just too much fresh air.

The underlying truth of my decision was, I didn't want anyone to invalidate the thoughts or feelings I was having. It was just so nice to walk around feeling like I was in love with the world. I am quite sure everyone saw a change in me that day, but most, probably just thought I was getting settled in. But that was just the beginning of the experiences I was to have in that two week time period. That was truly the proof I needed in my own mind that there are other life forms out there. Not only do they exist on other planets, but they also exist in other dimensional planes of reality. Science can't necessarily find what is out there because up until this point they are only searching within the confines of the third dimension.

Over the course of the next ten days that followed, not only myself, but most others that were there taking this course on this magical property had some form of Alien encounter. There were all types of encounters. Not all of them were as magical as my experience, but they were all powerful to the individual having the experience. There were times when we were in session I would glimpse the man who had come to visit me walking around the room bathed in this blue light that shone like an electric fog, silently touching people with the love that was as real in him as our hands are to us. Seeing him was very reassuring for me.

After a couple of days had passed even though I knew my experience to be real I guess it is the human part of me to second guess myself. Those thoughts I had of, did that really happen or not, started to creep in. Maybe it was just my imagination But once I saw him again I knew it had been real. The best thing however, was that I knew it could be real again. I somehow knew he had given me this gift to be able to share with the rest of humanity. To know that, this kind of love can be exchanged between all people keeps my faith in love alive.

The experience I had with him taught me that everything is connected. Every thought I have affects everyone. Everything I do sends a shock wave around this planet that will hit everyone in its wake. It is because of this that I try to live as positively as possible. I truly know that we are all based in love, and because of that we have the ability to change the anger, fear and frustration that sometimes seems to rule the planet into the one thread that runs through all of us. That thread is a living energy called love. The last day of the course was an extremely emotional day for all of us. Out of strangers we had found friends, and out of pain we had created peace. None of us wanted to leave. I knew that life could never be the same for me now. The experiences I had gone through, the lessons I had learned I could never again see the world as a lonely place.

The world I now knew was a wondrous place filled with adventure and beauty. It did not exist just on one dimensional level but was totally interactive on all dimensional levels, all you had to fo was open your eyes to see them. There was a big part of me that was nervous that I would not be able to function in the old world, perhaps people would see me as too different or I would see them as too normal. Then l realized people hadn't really understood me all my life, now wouldn't be so much different. So in one way nothing had changed. The only thing that had truthfully changed was me and my perceptions of the world around me. The theory of relativity had somehow come into conscious affect in my life. I guess it is true after all, that all perceptions are relative to the seer.

So I left my tent and my temporary home in Burks Falls that day not knowing what was going to happen in my life, but feeling that it wouldn't be dull and that I wouldn't be alone. Shedding a few tears, I drove away from the biggest turning point my life had seen. I was excited about going into the future, to an unknown destiny, but I also felt a huge loss for leaving the past behind. I knew that in leaving the past some people would also have to be left behind. The fear I had of Aliens had been greatly alleviated, but wasn't completely gone. Why, I was not sure. I did not know at that time that I was far from finished with Alien encounters. I could feel them around me now even stronger, but what I felt around me didn't feel the same as the man that had blessed me with his presence. The feeling that was around me was much harsher, more distant. and in some way hollow. At least that was the best I could describe it.

When I got home the house I had been living in was somehow different, almost as though it wasn't home anymore. There was a beautiful bouquet of flowers sitting on the table welcoming me, from a friend who's love I will always feel. The house looked exactly as I had left it, but something I could not explain, said I wouldn't be there much longer. This house had been my transitional place, and it had done its job well. It was now time for me to go on to the next segment of my life. So I opened my mind and my heart to discovering what lay ahead of me. If there was someone guiding me or helping me in some way, then please, let me know what I am to do next. I put that energy out there and it didn't take to long to bring results. Within two weeks I intuitively knew I had to go on a vision quest of sorts. My vision quest would take me out of the country. I had been shown in my heart that I was to start preparing for a journey into the United States. The particular place that seemed to be my destination was New Mexico.

That realization was a shock to me. I started to make preparations for my leaving. It didn't take long however for a certain state of reality to set in. I had no money, and my car was basically a wrecking yard reject. After I had made this decision to go, I kept running into people who would tell me about the tarantulas and scorpions that thrived in that part of the country and I was not fond of bugs.

And if it wasn't the bugs, they would have stories of the horrendous acts that human beings would do unto other human beings. Stories of horrendous violence. I don't know why people can't just say they had a wonderful time when they visited places like that. Instead they insist on telling you what a horrible place it is, and how a woman travelling alone will never survive. Encouragement came from very few people.

But I didn't seem to need it I just knew that if this journey was to happen, then everything would fall into place without too many complications. So slowly but surely I put one foot in front of the other and kept going in a focused direction. Time passed very quickly and I was realizing that I may not have enough money for the three month stay I had planned. So following the usual pattern of my nature I started saying to myself that perhaps I should back out and not go on this journey. Not enough money and too many people telling me that there was no way I would come home alive, slowly and surely people's words started diffusing the passion I had for this trip. So in an attempt to give myself a way of gracefully bowing out if I decided to cancel this adventure, I stated to myself that I needed a certain amount of money to be able to survive for three months and be able to return home safely.

I can't honestly say that I had the feeling that I wanted to get rid of everything I owned. Its important to understand at this point, I had worked a long time to furnish my home the way I wanted it. I had everything I needed to make my life comfortable, but in a split second I made the decision to sell everything I had worked years to be able to buy. And so the process started. Telling everyone I saw that all my possessions were for sale, putting an ad in the paper, and finally advertising the fact I was having the dreaded garage sale. It is truly amazing how many emotions get provoked when you do something like this. Going through all my old collectibles and trying to decide what was garbage and what was saleable. I remember so clearly watching the first piece of furniture that I was to sell go out the door. I really thought for a moment that I was going to have an anxiety attack.

For me, I think some how that was my first moment of real

commitment to a new life. After that it got easier. And so, after five long weeks, I decided to count the money I had saved and see where I was at. I knew I had one last pay coming to me, I started adding the figures and as I came to a total I started to laugh. The amount of money I had to start my vision quest with was exactly ten dollars more than I said I needed to have.

It is said that when you are meant to do something, everything comes together at just the right moment so you are able to accomplish the feat. Well that was the last sign I needed to convince me that what I was doing was the right thing to do, all I had to do now was say my good-byes and pack my car. In life, when you are dealing with a lot of people who do not have the same belief system as you do, things can get very confusing for loved ones that don't want to say good-bye because they can't or won't see your point of view. Many of the people I was saying bye to, were completely convinced that they would never see me again. Try as I may I couldn't make them understand that I just simply knew that I would be all right. I think these people knew on a subconscious level as well that after this trip my life would never be the same. So in some way the feeling of death that they felt was actually death of an old life, not death of a body. But they couldn't decipher the difference. So after a few tearful good-bye's and storing the couple of boxes I had to store, I packed my car and awaited the final moment of departure.

It was November 22 and there was already snow on the ground. It was crisp outside but not really cold. I stood leaning with my back up against the house, and somehow all the events of the last few months flashed before my eyes in a sequence that made sense to my being at this moment at this time. I knew I was ready to leave now, but I also knew I wasn't just leaving my home and my country. I knew I was leaving all perceptions of what life had been behind me. I had completed a cycle in my life and I was about to be re birthed into a new state of being. The only thing that made me nervous was, I just wasn't to sure what that new state of being was going to be.

Driving out of Canada was a completely new experience for me. The adrenaline that was running through my body was incredible. The biggest thing that I was looking forward to was getting out of the cold. I have never liked the cold weather. My body always feels as though it freezes up. Most of my travelling south was happening at night. I am one of those drivers that once I start travelling I don't want to stop until I reach my destination. Fortunately my first destination was North Carolina. So after driving for almost twenty two hours straight, I drove into Asheville. The climate was so warm and the mountains so beautiful it almost made me cry. I was to visit with friends here for a few days on my way to New Mexico.

But after being stationary for two days a huge feeling came over me that I had to go to Virginia Beach. So I packed up once again and made my way to the coast and to the ocean. I have loved the ocean and everything it represents for as long as I can remember. So driving into the beach area I could smell the salt in the air and feel the change from earth to water. Existence around the ocean is a state of constant change on a daily basis. With every rise in the tide, a new cycle starts. All life everywhere is always changing but somehow around the ocean it is exaggerated. So I arrived and found myself a motel room got settled and then as fast as I could I was down on the beach. Walking in the sand in your bare feet has got to be on of the best feelings your feet and your whole body can experience. The drawing that the sand creates to pull the toxins out of the body, it just leaves you feeling clean.

As I walked down the beach my attention was brought to the voices that I had been hearing in my head ever since I had crossed the border. Like light whisperings they were, like tiny little feathers of down were gently caressing my ears,the feeling was gently pulling me to the sea. For what l did not know but what I was beginning to sense was, the voices were getting louder and stronger. They still felt warm and gentle but there was more clarity now. I could make out actual sentence's and specific differences in certain voices. Walking in wet sand can tire you out very quickly especially if you aren't used to it. So even though the voices were compelling me I turned and walked back to my motel room. I crawled between the clean sheets and as quickly as I closed my eyes I was asleep.

Suddenly my eyes were open and they tried in vain to pierce the darkness. Searching for some point of light to focus on. There was no light but there was a presence, and then the voice, this was one of the voices that had become familiar to me on my trip. The voice seemed

28

to fill my body lifting it almost like a joyous melody had invaded my very being forcing it to move on its own. I stood and walked silently through the darkness until I could here the sound of gently rolling waves. The damp cool breeze brushed up against my cheeks creating a sharp contrast to the pillow I had just been laying against. Then and only then did I begin to see any light at all. It seemed faint and distant but it was brilliant and luminous, and as it moved there was a glow that seemed to follow it. As it came closer I could see the cresting of the waves on the water. I thought of how completely beautiful this movable moon was as it lingered just inches above the water. It was at this point that it dawned on me that this light was actually moving.

That's when the fear suddenly set in again I could feel that feeling of absolute panic that I would have, laying in bed at night waiting for the ships to come and take me .Even though the fear was there, I was mesmerized by the light. It seemed almost to pulsate. I thought I could see movement within that stationary glow. It was as though there was a top spinning within a delicate luminous mist. Stunned in amazement but chained by fear I stood unable to move no more than to breathe. As I watched this hovering wonder, the colour of its coat began to change, and within the mist the spinning movement began to slow down to a stop. My heart started to race, I thought this is it, I am going to die.

At that moment I became aware of a beautiful high pitched tone that seemed to emanate from the water itself. As my perceptions changed from the air to the water I saw what seemed to be hundreds of dolphins gathering in a spiral pattern surrounding this airborne object.. The dolphins were in sync singing some kind melody. As they sung I felt as though I was being cradled in joy and peace. I closed my eyes so that I could fully experience the feeling move through my body. Within seconds I sensed a change in the light that was before me, slowly I opened my eyes. From what I could see now, there was a beam of light being projected from the ship. The song that the dolphins had been singing had transformed itself from tones into a chorus of voices. These voices were the voices that I had been hearing in my head.

As the beam of light started to move across the water individual dolphins would come into the centre where the light was most intense. As they did this, their bodies would be lifted from the water. By the time they were fully clear of the surface of the water, they were no longer in the bodies of a dolphin. They were in an upright shape of an indiscernible form. They were basically shimmering, vibrating energy.

Beautifully pulsating silver gold light. It was so bright you felt you should turn away from it because it would damage your eyes, but it was not harsh to look at, and it did not hurt the eyes. I am not sure how long a time had passed as I watched this process of dolphins leaving the water to enter the ship as energy. but it felt like an instant. All at once an overwhelming energy hit my body that came in the form of a voice.

As I listened to the same melodic format I had been hearing for days the voice started to answer the questions that were present in my mind. I heard the voice say, "You have been brought to this place at this time to witness a truth. What you are seeing is, who the dolphin really is. All things on this earth are only a manifestation of a line of energies. Whether those energies be from this planet or from other planets or dimensions. Earth is a form of meeting point for all places and dimensions. This is one of the reasons earth is so important in this time frame. All places that have invested lines of energies onto earth have something to gain by the shift in consciousness that is to come. Everything you see, or know to be real to you is a contribution from somewhere else. It is now time for the humans of earth to know and understand the responsibility that they accepted in agreeing to be born at this time. We are preparing for a great jump in evolution. There is no right or wrong but there is positive and negative. The positives want a change toward love. The negatives want a change toward control. It is a part of the evolution of all of us. At this point none of us can go anywhere without the human. The human is a free will being. We cannot make any choices for you all we can do is answer your questions and allow you to make your own decisions. You need to see with your own eyes that nothing ever dies, it only changes to a form that is closer to its truth. Earth is in the process of creating a new truth, and we are here as a line of positive energy to answer your questions and activate you on your own individual path. We have come in the form of the dolphin because we exist in the water element. You know the water element to represent the emotional level. We have evolved to a level on which we live our entire existence through the emotional sea."

"As we swim these seas in our dolphin form, we are not just cutting a path through water. We are in fact moving through the tears of the earth. The tears she has cried for the love she feels for her children. This is why the water levels are rising. She cries more now as chaos approaches, she wishes the people could see what they are doing so she would not have cleanse herself. The earth, she cries for the pain we all feel. As you feel, she feels. She can only reflect where the mass consciousness is at any time. Do not blame the governments for the financially destitute situation, or the chemical companies for the ecological destruction. If you want to see where the real problem lies, look in the mirror. Do you really love yourselves, or is it easier to sabotage and destroy yourselves? Nothing will happen on this planet if you keep looking for your neighbour to change their ways. Perhaps your neighbour needs to see change is possible before he can have the faith that he can do it to. You set the example for earth, you are where change starts. You are the still point in the universe." With that each individual dolphin sent a beam of light back to the ship. The next thing I knew I was back in my motel room.

It was morning and the sunlight was streaming through the windows. I got up, got dressed and went to get a coffee. As I wandered down the slowly awakening streets, I thought the world somehow looked different to me than it had the night before. I walked into the closest coffee shop and hoped the coffee was drinkable although I don't think it would have mattered at that point. While I was waiting to get my coffee I spoke to the waiter about the dolphins that were around here, and how there seemed to be so many of them. The waiter looked back at me quite shocked and wanted to know where I had seen so many dolphins at this time of year. As I returned his gaze, he couldn't help but see my confusion. It seems the dolphins generally leave that area for warmer waters in September, and it was now the end of November.

"The end of September", I thought, how was that possible? I saw them with my own eyes. A little confused and concerned, I walked back to my motel room. All the way I puzzled over what the waiter had said. If the dolphins leave at the end of September, did I imagine what I had seen the night before. It was still early in the morning and as I walked towards my room I kept getting the feeling that I was going in the wrong direction. I knew where I was, but my body was pulling me in the direction of the ocean. So I thought that maybe it was a good idea if I went for a stroll along the beach before I got busy with my day. I probably walked two miles before deciding to return to the motel. When I got back more than three hours had passed but that didn't matter as I had no where I had to be anyway. I sat down on the edge of the bed and turned on the television. I checked out what was happening in the area to see if there is a spot I needed to visit. After a few minutes of watching the local agenda, the thought of a nap became most appealing. So I turned off the television and lay down, as I closed my eyes I thought I heard the whispering starting in my ears once again. But within seconds I was asleep.

Virginia Beach is such a magical place. It is very tourist oriented. All the buildings are brightly coloured and there is a wide variety of entertainment. There always seems to be something going on somewhere, and then you have all the military bases in the area. So no matter what, there is always some kind of movement happening. I spent a few days there in the ocean energies and just generally recuperating in my own personal way. For most of the time I was there, I heard the voices. Sometimes they were close, and sometimes they were far away but they seemed to be there at all times, night and day. There were far too many messages passed to me to remember them individually. Some of them were important on a world wide basis, others were for me personally. But all messages seemed to come from the beings I had known as dolphins.

I left Virginia Beach within the week, and as I drove away, back to North Carolina, I thought of how I never again would be able to think of dolphins as just being animals ever again. I wondered how many people on this earth had the opportunity to see what I had seen? How many people new the truth? Why couldn't the dolphins just let everyone know who they were? But the biggest question on my mind was about my own fear. Is it possible that I had been afraid of the dolphin beings? Or was it something else? I am sure my trip into the beach area was meant to answer some questions for me, but all it really did was create more.

Within a few short hours I was back in North Carolina. I stayed there a couple of days and met some new people, but that little nagging feeling of movement crept up on me again and I new it was time to go. So I said good bye to my new friends and my old friends and I headed out for New Mexico. I had never done much travelling in the U.S.A., so I was all eyes, discovering the unfamiliar territory and landscapes. There is some breathtakingly beautiful scenery on the route I took to get where I was going. My senses were overwhelmed with all the newness that I was discovering. I crossed the New Mexico border within a day and a half. I can honestly say that I was exhausted from driving and I wasn't used to the elevation. The landscapes I travelled were like watching the creation of a masterpiece.

The colours of the soil and the jagged formations of the mountains made me feel more like I was on another planet, not just in another country. Fascinated and definitely intimidated by the grandeur that was before me, I decided to pull into Las Vegas and take a motel for the night. As I parked my vehicle and took my bag into the room, I was realizing how dizzy I was from the elevation. It was almost the feeling you get when you have had too much too drink and your head starts to swim. Even though the sensation was a little disorienting it was almost pleasurable. I love the different natural sensations that life brings you. I tend to enjoy the experience of heightened perception in my physical body, but I have found that the experience has to be natural and not substance induced to be valid.

After sitting in my motel room for awhile I could feel my body adjusting to the new pressures in the air. Feeling better, I decided to take a walk and see some of the town. As I walked through the streets I got the feeling of history. This place was very old and had been inhabited by people for a very long time. It didn't take long before I started to get that feeling of dizziness in my head again. I headed back for the motel and decided to check in with home and just let them know that everything was all right and I was still very much alive.

With all this accomplished I put my head down to rest as I watched the local news. I think I must have fallen asleep instantly. I awoke in absolute panic! That is all I could feel. I went to try and move my body but I couldn't . What's wrong? I could hear noise in the room but I couldn't seem to locate it. Oh, right the television is on. Wait there is movement in here. I am not alone! Oh God I feel dizzy. Who are those little people? What are the doing? My body feels funny. What's going on? I don't understand what's happening here. I want to sleep. Leave me alone. And then everything fell silent.

I don't know how much time had passed before I woke myself up again, but that feeling of panic was still very strong. Then I started remembering what I had seen. There were people in my room. Immediately I jumped up to check my possessions and see if they were still there. All my stuff was still there, nothing even looked as though it has been touched. Why would anyone be in my room and not steal my stuff? I know thieves do look for specific things, and I had some things with me that were worth money as well. All I knew at this point was I didn't feel safe. I don't like it when I cant answer questions in a way that my mind can make peace with. And when I don't feel safe I wont stay in the place that I am in. So I packed up and left Las Vegas in the middle of the night. I can't say it made me feel any safer being on the road driving, but at least I wasn't in one spot.

Morning came and I was in Sante Fe. This is such a beautiful place. As you drive into Sante Fe, you are engulfed by mountains and they draw all your attention to them. Then all of a sudden you round a bend and there before you is this beautiful little town at the bottom of a valley. Sante Fe is a very cultural community. You can feel the Native and Mexican vibration, but there is such a wide variety of people that live here now it is truly a multi cultural community. I spent the whole day in the city meeting people. The people here I found to be very pleasant, however this is also a very transient place. People come here all the time and cant take the vibration for long so they push on to their next destination. And for all I was worth, even though I thought this was to be my destination, I could not see myself staying here. The city didn't seem to have a central state of time, everyone seemed to move on their own time. I found Sante Fe to be very beautiful but also very confusing to me. So I left and headed south. Not sure of where I was going or even what I was doing. I just knew I had to follow my instincts and they said not to stay here in

Sante Fe.

   As I travelled I became more concerned that perhaps this trip was all in vain. I didn't know where I was going. I felt that my intuition had failed me. What I had thought was going to happen did not, so what was I going to do now. I just kept going south and then I turned west, I ended up in Rock Hound New Mexico. For some reason this little park really attracted me and so I decided to stay. I set up camp at the top of the hill. I love the feeling of being able to overlook the landscape below. There is something about being able to see as far as the eye can see that I find very exciting.

   One thing that really impacted me about this part of the world was the night skies. The contrast between the stars and the deep midnight blue color that the sky becomes after dark is beyond stunning. It literally took my breath away just staring into the celestial heavens at night, but it also made me realize how far away I was from home. The stars are in a very different pattern here than they are in my part of the world. This somehow led to a slightly eerie feeling and in some ways added to the fear I already felt around the Alien issue. The first night I stayed there I drifted off to sleep almost in a state of hypnosis simply by watching the stars move through the deep blue waves of velvet.

   This state park is totally set up for people who want to go rock hunting. Many people come here and scavenge the hillside for minerals or dinosaur eggs or whatever else they can find. It is an excellent pastime and a great way to get some exercise. So I decided to do the same. Not that I was looking to collect rocks but I thought that some exercise would do me some good and maybe clear my head.

   As I climbed to the top of the mountain I could feel the sun on my face and the gentle breeze that was blowing across my body. For the first time in the last few days I felt some peace. I just sat at the top of the this hill surveying my surroundings and something caught my attention out of the corner of my eye. As I turned to look at what it was, I thought I would stop breathing. There right in front of me was a large disc shaped object descending below the outline of the mountain. I didn't know what to do. I wanted to run but my legs wouldn't move. The fear I had been dealing with for the last while was now right in front of me. The disc just kept descending until all of a sudden the earth seemed to shimmer for a mere second and the disc then disappeared below the surface. I shook my head in an attempt to see if it was really there or not. After all the sun was hot and I was lonely and I was in unfamiliar territory. My logical mind was once again racing for a reasonable answer, but I was just grasping at straws. Nothing but the fact that I had just seen a real live UFO made any sense.

As soon as I could move I went back down the hill. It felt as though I were moving very quickly even though I wasn't. My perceptions were all messed up for the moment. I wanted to get out of there, but I knew I was not really capable of driving. So I had no choice but to wait. I decided to stay for one more night. But I also promised myself that I wouldn't sleep and I would watch the sky all night for a sign of these things showing themselves once more. I think I made it until three in the morning and then I fell asleep. That night all I dreamed of, was ships flying through the air. In my dreams it felt as though I was flying some of the ships myself and in others I was just along for the ride. I liked that feeling of flying it was so free, I have never liked being confined to the ground

In the morning I left and kept heading straight west. I think I cried for an hour because I didn't know where I was going. I was stressed with fear and all alone. But as I approached the Arizona border the dark cloud that hung over me seemed to disperse and lift. When I came in range of Tucson, I knew beyond any doubt this was going to be home for me for the rest of my time in the U.S.A. My thoughts were validated as I pulled within the city limits as a giant rainbow crossed the sky and there wasn't a single cloud to be seen. I had found home and my heart was happy.

The desert itself is an amazing experience, but Tucson was like an entire city founded in suburbia. As I drove around just trying to orient myself I was astounded by the way the city is spread out over an extended area. I assumed that it had something to do with the desert and the fragile ecosystem that exists within it. Thoughts of a desert usually bring a vacant wasteland to mind, but in truth the high desert is very alive. Everywhere there were birds and animals. The overruling colour is beige, but even within the beige there is green.

This place was warm and dry, which is just perfect for my physical composition. I am a water sign, so cold can really leave me feeling sluggish. But the warmth here, even though it was December, made me feel reborn. I knew I was going to love it here.

Tucson like Sante Fe is a very diverse society. My first few days of moving around and mingling with people left me to discover that almost no one was born and raised in the city, but instead had relocated here from a colder climate or they had come in from the California coast. I am very accustomed to this type of situation. The place where I am from is a traditional sort of tourist town. Most of the people that are there have moved in from other places to either retire or start up small businesses. Any of the people that were born there that still reside there, tend to move out of town only to return at a later date. It is one of those home towns that people have a hard time staying away from.

Everyone seemed to love Tucson though, and it also seemed to be a place of extremes. people had very definite opinions on things. There seemed to be no Gray areas. Another thing I noticed was that this seemed to be another area of high military concentration. The air force is located right in the city itself and just south of here in the Huachuca mountains was the army. I was starting to wonder why I was being drawn to areas of high military concentration, but I could figure that out later. For now I just wanted to get settled somewhere. I thought I would look for a room to rent instead of staying in motels. That can get pretty expensive. One thing I have learned from the travels I have had in my life is that if you really want to experience the culture of a place, then you must plop yourself right in the middle of it. For me that would mean living in the house of a local.

So I sat down and tried to think about what I was doing in this place. I was on some kind of vision quest. A learning experience that was based in a higher state of consciousness. So for me to learn whatever it was that I was to learn I must look for people that have like minds. So the next logical step for me to take would be to find some spiritual bookstores. So one Sunday afternoon I looked in the phone book and found what I was looking for. It usually doesn't take me long to orient myself in a new place. I was beginning to see that maybe that was why I spent three years of my life driving a taxi cab.

There is no better way to learn how to drive, or to learn about dealing with people than to drive a cab. So that job came in very handy now that I was travelling so much. I bought a map, and within minutes was on my way to finding and establishing a new temporary address.

Tucson had three major Spiritual bookstores when I first arrived. As I made my rounds, trying to become a familiar face and checking out the availability of rooms I saw that so many of the books on the shelves had something to do with Aliens. Many of the books that were here, I had never even seen in Canada. I was fascinated by the interest that there seemed to be in the world of the unknown down here.

There seemed to be an open and adventurous spirit in discovering the unknown here. I was really beginning to see that I could fit into this place more than I had ever fit in anywhere before. I had located two of the listings in the phone book and thoroughly enjoyed both stores. But the listing I was most interested in locating still seemed to elude me. I had been to the street address and still could not find the place. I thought that perhaps it had gone out of business until I saw a newly published ad featuring it. I returned to the same address twice with no luck so I decided to try once more and if I still had no luck I would not return.

However on the third pass I found the place tucked away in the corner of the mall where I had not previously looked. It was a beautiful large store with lots of space and a lecture hall. There were some other smaller rooms for meditation and tarot reading. But what fascinated me the most was, this place's main focus was on Aliens.

My whole life seemed to be focusing itself around Aliens. No matter where I went there were these strange beings in front of me. I knew this could not be a coincidence. So I accepted the direction of fate and introduced myself to the people at the Blue Millennium. Little did I know what a powerful impact this place was going to have on my life .

The people here were very much a mixed bag from all walks of life. However their purpose seemed to be singular. These people had given themselves over to help others overcome their fear of Aliens.

They were all very qualified within their own fields of expertise. All had been through some kind of encounter or experience with these other worldly beings. Their viewpoints varied from the logical analytical to the spiritual. But in any case I was fascinated by the commitment these people had as a group to help the mass amounts of people that were struggling with some form of fear. For some reason it never dawned on me that I was here for the same reason, to process the fear I felt around Aliens, I thought I just really liked the people and the atmosphere. I am quite sure now that I must have had Alien experience written all over me as I walked through that door the first time.

As I spoke with the owner I mentioned that I read tarot and she asked if I would do a reading for her. I did and I ended up doing readings for all the staff members that were either employed by or volunteered at the Blue Millennium. This somehow cemented the fact that I was about to become one of the family members here in this place. A sense of family was exactly what I needed now that I was so far away from home.. Within days I had established a certain role with my new found family structure and I had also found a physical place to live with one of the regulars who frequented the store.

So I packed up my stuff and moved into a small apartment with a warm caring woman in her forties who was very spiritual and was originally from California. This was to be my home for awhile and space was tight but we both shifted ourselves to make the best of the room that was available. I guess this is really where my experiences started. I was spending a lot of time at the Blue as it came to be known. This was such a strange world for me. I had never really been exposed to topics such as UFO's and conspiracy's before. But it was when the conversations turned towards the abduction issue that I tended to walk away or drift off in another direction. It was almost as though I would start to dissociate the minute I heard the word abduction. I, like most people don't deal with fear from a head on approach. I kind of like to come at it from different angles until it's not looking and then sneak up and attack it. For the first little while the time I spent at the Blue would totally exhaust me. The energy drain was incredible. Of course I didn't recognize it as denial of my own situation, so I just put it down to adjusting to a new climate. But it wasn't long before something started to happen inside of me that was just like having a thorn in your side. There was something that was constantly nagging at me. A feeling that I should know something or remember something that I just couldn't quite recall.

Now when this type of feeling happens in me it is actually the curiosity that drives me to go beyond whatever fear lies within me. That need to know becomes all consuming. However in this case I wasn't sure what it was I needed to know. I could just feel the approach of some kind of information that would forever change my perception of existence. Another thing that was confusing me was some of the physical reactions my body was having to what I thought was this new climate. I didn't understand how dry the desert really was when I first arrived in Tucson.. One of my biggest problems is that I am not a big water drinker. So within a couple of weeks of being here, dehydration set in.

Being dehydrated is really an unusual feeling. Its like you are sick and you're not. You can feel dizzy and nauseated all at the same time. But instead of having the flu you just don't have enough fluid in your body. So as I was going through this I was also experiencing some severe tingling in my body especially at night. I just put this down to being part of the dehydration even though I knew that the feeling of pins and needles was rather unusual. It was always the same, it would start at the feet and move over my whole body so that it would leave me virtually paralysed. It always seemed to happen just as I was falling asleep. As I monitored the pattern. t discovered that the nights this happened my dream state would also be overly bizarre. So allowing for the need to explain everything logically, I just watched what was happening to my body from a neutral place and thought that all these annoying little problems would disappear in a couple of weeks after I settled into the climate and circumstances. After all, I had been through a huge amount of change in a relatively small amount of time. So I told myself not to worry about things needlessly and I went on about my business of trying to learn more about this amazing new world I found myself in.

Days passed and I did get over the dehydration. But these other symptoms were still with me. What finally did it for me was when bruises started appearing on my body in very strange places. I would have a bruise on my ankle in the morning that looked half healed that hadn't been there the night before. Strange little marks on my body that looked like skin had been removed but yet they looked as though they were almost healed. This pushed me beyond my considerable ability to explain the unexplainable. I had to find out what was going on, even though I knew I didn't really want the answer.

I don't know which is worse. Knowing what you are afraid of, and still being afraid of it, or being afraid and not knowing the cause. But terror is something that can consume your life. Fear can actually be like an addiction. If you can name your fear that is one thing, but when fear runs you, that is when it becomes like an addiction. Far too many times, I have experienced fear as an addiction. In some ways using fear as a hiding place in my life so that I wouldn't have to do something I didn't want to, or progress in my life. Fear can be that place that you go to as an excuse not to have to be who you really are. And so I decided to approach what I considered to be the experts in this fear. I went to the people who were quickly becoming my family, the people of the Blue. I spoke with Gina the owner. I told her of my fears and of the things that had been happening to me.

She said that she had assumed as much. There is always an energy to people that have been having abduction experiences. Once you train yourself to recognize the energy, you can spot it immediately. In some ways it is almost as though there is a foreign energy that is trying to intrude in the field that surrounds your being. She did a little feeling around my head in specific spots. She was feeling along the base of the skull. Then suddenly she stopped. The look on her face changed to one of concern. Of course this made me feel even more like panicking so basically I looked at her and yelled "What!" Gina looked at me with compassion, understanding my state of stress.

One thing that took me by surprise is that as she spoke there was no trace of shock or disapproval in her voice. Nothing in her words told me that this was unusual or bizarre even though what she told me was beyond my ability to comprehend at first. What she said was this, she spoke of Aliens, she called them the Greys. She said they had been here on earth for a few years now. They have been doing genetic experiments with human beings. No one seemed to be sure what the experiments were about exactly but it seemed to be happening to a lot of people all over the world. I told her I was aware of the abduction experience, I had seen the movie Communion. Communion is a movie about the experiences of a man by the name of Whitley Streiber and the changes he goes through after learning that he has been involved with the Greys all his life. It deals in depth with his supposed paranoia, and the disbelief of everyone around him. She then asked me how it had made me feel. I told her that I was unable to finish the whole movie because it had terrified me. She said in a calm firm voice that whether I remembered or not, she felt that I had been abducted and there was one other thing. Well, that was my cue to head straight for denial. Immediately I said "no I don't think so" even though there was part of me that knew she was right. Then she dropped the bombshell. She talked of a tiny little unit that could be injected under the skin and left there, so the Aliens could constantly monitor the owner of the unit. It was not known for sure why they use these devices, but it was assumed it was just to monitor bodily functions on a daily basis. Well talk about going into overload the next thing I really remember, I was in my car on my way home.

My mind was racing looking for some kind of safe space something that would wake me up so I could dismiss this as a nightmare. The word "Implant" just kept going through my mind. How dare these things whatever they are, intrude on my life. How was this happening to me? I mean, I might be naive but I am not stupid. Then I started to wonder about the people I was now calling friends. Maybe they were all crack pots? Maybe I was getting myself involved in some sort of cult or something. After all, enough people told me that I was going to get into trouble doing this trip by myself. Maybe they were right after all.

When I got home no one was there. For this I was thankful right now I felt as thought I needed to be alone, to think this thing through without anyone's influence. My biggest question right now was, could this really be happening? These people had no reason to lie to me, maybe they just had Aliens on the brain so much, that everyone they saw was some kind of victim? I thought myself to death for several hours. I must of exhausted myself because, I was overcome with tiredness and could no longer stress myself out while conscious. I fell into a deep sleep which is exactly what I was trying to avoid.

All I remember from the dream state is this, I was walking along what seemed to be a dirt road. Then all of sudden the whole sky was full of disc shaped objects, there seemed to be hundreds of them. I was terrified, I started to run, but there was no where to go. All of a sudden all of these beams of energy started to hit me, pulling me off the ground towards one huge central disc. But then out of nowhere a man appeared right in front of me. This is a man I have seen for years now. I have come to consider him some kind of guide or assistant in life. He blocked the beam of energy so that I was no longer being pulled toward the ship. He looked directly into my eyes and told me to go beyond my fear because there was a purpose in my doing so. Then as quickly as he had appeared, he was gone. And with him went all the ships that I had seen there just a second before.

So even though I wasn't sure whether I believed in Aliens or not, I knew I had to face my fears. whether the fear was of Aliens or of something else really didn't matter. The fact was, fear is fear and it needs to be dealt with. So with a very queasy feeling in my stomach I decided to talk to Gina tomorrow and see what could be done to solve this little problem.

The next time I went into the Blue the first thing Gina said to me was she wasn't sure if I was going to come back or not. I acknowledged the fact that I had entertained that thought, but the truth was more important to me than my own fears. I tried to explain that what was being talked about, with all the abductions and implants and stuff was pretty much a stretch even for my imagination. I had to ask her if she really believed in all that stuff or was she trying to stir up business for her store. What she did was tell me her story. She had worked at an airport and never really gave any thought to Aliens or anything of that nature. But she started talking to pilots and hearing their stories of seeing objects in the sky. She also heard how the stories were stopped in their tracks. But even though she heard the stories she really wasn't, sure what to believe. Then one day she had an experience in her own home with an Alien. That convinced her of their existence. But part of her experience was to learn that the abductions can be stopped simply by saying "no" to these beings.

This is something people in general didn't know. She felt totally compelled to do what she could to help people through these bizarre sets of circumstances. After all this is not exactly something that is recognized by the public let alone accepted. This is the kind of stuff they lock you up and throw away the key for.

After I heard that, I can honestly say I did feel more comfortable, not so much with my situation, but with the people I was putting my vulnerabilities in the hands of. So now the next step was to find out the process I needed to go through to stop this from happening anymore. Even then I wasn't so sure that I was convinced it was happening. I was told all I had to do was say no to the experience! Well how could I say no when I never remembered it happening? So Gina told me to start programming my mind to be conscious and awake through the experience so I could say no. I really didn't like the idea of that. I wasn't too sure I wanted to remember. So the next thing she said to me was, "don't let this stuff intimidate you". She told me to get it through my head that I was in control. I had to be totally convinced or even totally angry at being intruded upon. Anger was the angle I needed to work from. I could feel that rage in me. Who were these beings to think they could do whatever they wanted to me? And that was another question I wasn't sure if I wanted answered or not. What were they doing to me? I felt that somehow there was a lot more to it than just simply being abducted.

So I started to consciously program my mind. I don't like feeling as though human beings have control over me, let alone some thing that doesn't have the fortitude to show itself and just wants to play with people's mind. I could feel myself getting angrier and angrier. I was at the point where I thought, just bring them on, and I'll take care of this once and for all. And so I waited. There was nothing else for me to do. Gina recommended that I read about the things that had happened to other people, but I am the kind that needs my experience to be pure. I have always felt that the knowing of other people's experiences might effect my mind by making me think something is happening that really isn't. Then one night my wait was over.

I had gone to bed and fell asleep very quickly because it had been a long day and I was very tired. I am really not sure how long I had been asleep for when all of a sudden I seemed to be dreaming. I was on a rooftop looking out at the night skies beyond the Catalina mountains and staring at the dramatic display of stars, when I noticed

44

two of the guys from the Blue were there with me. They just seemed to be talking and milling around doing whatever, but I could hear some kind of sound. It wasn't music, it was more like single tones being played in some kind of sequence. The tones were different than what you would hear on earth. They were clearer and more defined somehow. As I listened I found them to be almost mesmerizing. Then my programming must have activated itself because I was suddenly very conscious and awake no longer under the spell of the tones. As I looked ahead of me I could see lights approaching. I ran over to Seth and Bill and said they are here feeling like I was going to throw up from fear and excitement. But I could see that they were under the same influence of hypnosis that I had been under moments ago. This feeling of hypnosis was almost catching and I felt myself lapse for a moment. The next thing I knew I was in a room I can only describe as being very clinical. I was lying naked on a cold steel table. I was laying on my stomach and I could feel pressure as though something was being pushed into my back. I remember wondering where Seth and Bill were.

But then I thought about being conscious and I started to try and see who was holding me captive. What I saw startled me and I started thinking that this wasn't possible. They were small bodied beings with long skinny arms that seemed to move on their own without conscious muscle effort. The hands were oversized compared to the arms and something about their bodies made me think of a child. It was their face that really made fear penetrate my body. Somehow in a single instant I felt my entire life go through me. I felt myself at five years old being taken by the hand and lead to the ship by one of these beings, other time periods flashed before my eyes of moments when I had been on the ships. It was the eyes of these beings that triggered everything. Their head was huge as it sat on the top of their neck It looked as though it had been delicately balanced there. There was a tiny slit where a mouth should be. They didn't have a nose that protruded from their face as a human nose protrudes. Their eyes were huge and black. They were an extended almond shape and wrapped more than halfway around their head. I got the feeling that those eyes could see everything about you, there was nowhere to run or hide from those eyes. Very shortly after seeing their eyes I remembered the feeling of wanting to pass out and the next thing I knew I woke up in my bed gasping for air.

That sealed my fate for the night, I don't think I moved for the rest of the night. I just sat in my bed clutching my knees. I had backed myself up against the wall so that anything that came near me would have to come at me head on or come through the wall. My eyes got so sore from not wanting to blink because something might get me. It had long been daylight outside when I finally just fell over sleeping because of emotional stress. I guess I believed they couldn't get me during the daylight hours. I woke up a few hours later embarrassed at the way I had reacted. I was petrified and I knew I had not said no to these beings. My body had been paralysed with fear, and I guess that included my vocal chords. I was to embarrassed to go to the Blue and admit that I had failed in my mission, but even more I think I was embarrassed to admit that I hadn't fully believed anything Gina had told me. It was just to safe for me to think maybe she was telling me an amazing story. So for the rest of the evening, I sat trying to analyze what had realty happened to me. I tried to dismiss it in certain logical ways, but i couldn't. It was too real and I knew it.

So I let it be and decided to deal with it tomorrow. My denial was working to my advantage. I didn't sleep very well that night either but I didn't expect to considering all that had happened. My sleep was spotty until late into the morning, so it was mid day before I was able wake myself enough to feel like going into the Blue and talking to Gina. When I got there all she said was "It happened again, didn't it?" My first response was, "How did you know? All she said was you have that look. Instead of pursuing a response I just left it alone. I was at the point of not being sure how much I really wanted to know anymore. After all I was just a country girl from Canada, why was I getting in the middle of all this? I turned to talk to Gina, but the ever ringing phone demanded her attention before I could spit out the words I had to say. I was wandering around the store like a lost puppy, when a very strange man came in.

He looked at me immediately and started walking towards me. Something about this guy was very indescribable, he looked pretty average but it was the way he made me feel I guess, that put me on edge. He spoke to me friendly enough as he slowly circled me. Finally I asked him what he wanted. He simply responded with, "You are one of them." I didn't know what he meant, but fear exploded in me assuming he thought I was one of the Greys.

"What are you? Crazy or something. I'm no Alien" My temper was coming dangerously close to making itself known for the first time in years. Calmly now he asked me to sit down and talk with him because he thought he may have some information that I needed to know if I was going to keep communicating with these beings. I was tired of fighting this thing anymore. My life had become so strange that maybe some stranger off the street could give me answers that I had travelled over thirty five hundred miles to find. If not, then this guy was just crazy and maybe I was crazy to. It takes one to know one and all that. So I conceded and invited the gentleman into the little room at the end of the main showroom.

Even after we sat down and he couldn't physically walk around me anymore, his eyes still penetrated me in a way that I have never experienced. It was as though he saw me as an immortal energy instead of just a human being. I sat there quietly trying to compose myself, I opened my mouth to offer my name, he just raised his hand in a gesture that told me he didn't want to know. He then seemed to almost melt into his chair and his eyes got a far away look to them and his shape looked as though it was starting to change. As this was happening, I can only describe what I saw, by saying, that it looked like a hologram had appeared as an overlay on top of his body. I found myself unable to move as I watched this mesmerizing energy swirl around his body starting to settle into some kind of a formation. It looked just like coloured air in motion.

As the motion of the energy around him slowed to a stop he gently started to speak. I am not really human, yes I look as though I am but I am not You noticed me the minute I walked into this space. You were not sure what it was that you noticed but something wasn't as you are accustomed to. I knew when I saw you, who you were. Do you know who you are?"

All I could do was shake my head no. All my life, all I had wanted was to know who I was, or what I was doing here, and now it was being offered to me and I wasn't sure I really wanted to know. It was then I realized this being in front of me was totally telepathic. Again he spoke, " I understand your fears in knowing who you are. Once you know, your life will never be the same. You will have to accept the responsibility for who you are and what you know. It will be hard for you to feel as though you fit here in this place called Earth. But always know that what you are doing here is a very important job. You are as I am, and in time you shall come to know this and accept it. I will now show you who you are."

As I stared at him unable to speak or even blink I watched as the energy around him started to move and shift once again into a new pattern. As it stilled itself, I felt tears begin to well up in my eyes. For what I saw in front of me was what I had feared I sat looking into the huge black eyes of one of the Greys. I am not that thing, I could feel my anger erupting to the surface again. How dare this man or thing or whatever it is accuse me of being one of those things?

I was a human being and nothing could change that. He could feel the level of stress that I was approaching and so he quickly shifted back to the human form that he had entered the store in. As he looked at me I could see the compassion in his eyes for me. Those things were from another place in space and time. I can't be in two places at one time. I was grasping to understand anything that would make sense in that moment.

"I understand your sense of desperation, I too, once felt as you feel this very moment. Several years ago a man came to me and took me out of the safety of my dulled senses into a place of truth. Sometimes we feel as though the truth can be harsh, but it really is freedom. For in truth lies power, the power of discovering ourselves, and once we discover ourselves there is nothing that can stop us from being who we are. Truth is power, power is freedom, freedom is love, and love is truth. This is the one sequence that reigns true through all dimensions. This is the sequence that you are about to start living in your life. So even though the fear you feel now is justified in your mind, it is also your illusion. To get beyond the illusion, you must feel your truth This is why you have come to this place at this time. The beings that you call the Greys are not what you think they are. and this must become part of your truth if you are to make a change on this planet. You call what they do, abducting against your will. They call what they do survival. They do not perceive existence in the same way that you do. So much is left for you to learn and accept. You will have the opportunity to interact with the Greys many times.

There is no need for you to go through the typical interaction with them that most people experience. These beings need your help as much as you need theirs, whether you believe this yet or not. Go gracefully with these people when they come for you. offer them your help and what you shall gain will be invaluable to you in the times to come. Work with them as you would with any stranger from a foreign land. Allow them the same courtesy you would desire. They are not necessarily more powerful than you just because you think they come from another planet. Remember, if they had the power that human beings try to give them, they would not even be here. Remember always, that all things that occur in our lives act as our mirrors."

Because you perceive these beings as Aliens, universal laws do not change. Perhaps all the people that are so terrified of them, or that have had such horrendous experiences of pain and intrusion should look at their lives and ask why they are mirroring such events in their lives. If their experience was one of pain, maybe they should stop to wonder if they can deal with the pain there already is in their own earthly lives. Without pain in their Earthly lives the Greys could not give them pain in an abduction experience."

I hated to admit it, but this guy was making some kind of sense to me on a level that I could feel but not rationalize. He was right. Universal laws of non-intrusion exist if you know enough to apply them. But who this man was I did not know, and why was he here with me?

"Who I am is not important, the message I carry is. You will be in a position to help many people lose their fears. you are to teach universal laws and how to apply them to help create the new earth. Remember what I am about to tell you now, even if you remember nothing else of our time together, the new earth is coming humans have given this event a name. They call it the shift. This shift is perceived to create chaos on earth, through earthquakes storms, and other natural disasters. This may not necessarily be what is going to happen. You must open your mind now to truth. This way you will know and understand what is to be, so that you can assist the masses through this process. Many unusual things will happen over the next twenty years. You must see from a place of truth to know what is real and what is the illusion that some will try to create. Not all will be wiling to let go of the control that they think they now have. If you look from a place of truth you will maintain the power to keep your freedom and therefore find your place of peace and this peace you feel will create an impenetrable shield around you and this shield is called love. Nothing will be able to touch you or those that you love if you do this.. I leave you now to think of what I have said and to make your decision."

With that he was gone. I never again saw him at least not yet. But sometimes I have the feeling that he is watching me from some place high above. After that I was so tired all I could think of was sleeping. I made my excuses for leaving and I went home to bed. On the way home I could feel my paralysing fears diminishing but as of yet I did not know why.

Chapter Four

I can honestly say that I could feel what this being had to say more than understand what he was saying. I knew all the indicators were there for world chaos, but it is something that you try not to think about on a daily basis. After the meeting with this person I somehow knew what he said to be be a reality. I felt suspended, I could feel my body but it was numb. It was as though my thoughts were moving too fast for me to pay any attention to my body. All that night I just lay in my bed. I felt unable to move. I could only think. I was able to see that my life was changing with every breath I took. The only thing I wasn't sure of was, if I was ready to meet the challenge of the change. Anyone who is not considered part of what society perceives as normal usually has a very difficult time in life and I had been labelled unusual so much, it was my normal. The ideas I had running through my mind definitely went beyond the boundaries that normal would define. I was thinking in a manner that was so unfamiliar to me I stopped to wonder if it was really me that was having the thoughts. I had somehow stopped thinking on an individual level, and started seeing everything as an event that affected the whole planet and the whole universe. In this pattern of thought I was able to think of a common occurrence such as taking your first step when you are a baby, and link it to my age and then seeing a pattern form in my life where I had a chance to take a new step every thirteen months of my life.

I was able to see how the state of emotional stability in a country formed the economic status, the health factors, and even, the weather patterns. But the most powerful vision I had in my head at that time was of the earth itself. I saw earth as she looks now, but I also saw her as an energy being.

To put a picture in your mind of what I saw just think of earth covered in multi coloured columns of light that look like porcupine quills of different sizes. Earth was completely covered in what appeared to be beams of light that came either from the centre of her being or they were being beamed to her surface from somewhere in space. I have never seen anything even remotely similar to this in a photograph.

Each one of these beams had its own colour and its own frequency of vibration. The colours ranged from black to pure white and everything in between. It was as though this was earth's aura. You could tell where the happy and sad places were. You could see where there was disease and unrest. But you could also tell where there was a place of beauty. But just as I became accustomed to looking at this bizarre giant porcupine, all the points of light and colour changed in what seemed to be the unlocking of some kind of astral puzzle box. All the points of light had moved to a new spot. Some had even changed their colour.

I knew when I looked at this I was seeing the future of earth and the locking in of the new grid system that is attached to the magnetic field that surrounds earth.

Wait a minute! l knew exactly what I was thinking about, but I also realized that until that moment I didn't even know earth had a magnetic field that looked like that. I was tempted to call it the morphomagnetic field because of the way it moved and shifted. I could see how each individual person on this planet will be pulled toward the beam of light that they most closely vibrate to. That is why people all over the world are in such a state of movement. One of the most common statements in the last ten years has to be, "I'm trying to find where I belong." So many people are searching for what feels like home to them so that they can put down some roots. People are starting to feel pushed to get where they have to be so that when the shift happens they are ready to meet the fate of their future. People must complete the karmic requirements of this lifetime and to do so they may have to move. I could also see that some of the power places on earth would fade only to be replaced by new ones that would be created with the conjunction of new meridian lines in relatively unknown areas. So many of the people that continue in their pilgrimages to the famous, sacred and spiritual spots around the world may no longer be getting that special energy boost that they journey there for, and if they do not follow their instincts as to where the new power lies, they may never find it. I lay thinking about all this for a very long time. How was I supposed to describe this to people? Would they believe me? This was something I could not worry about now. I was exhausted and before I knew it, sleep had taken me.

It seemed to be my fate in Tucson to be in more than one home. I was to move three times while I was there, and I now found myself preparing for the last move. I didn't have a clue as to where I was going to end up this time. It seemed as though I had to move every time I changed the way I thought. I have known for a long time that nothing is truly stable, but I was getting tired of looking for a new home all the time. It's funny, by nature, I am the type that likes stability and a home base, but somehow in my life I have never been able to have one for long. So I started my regular tour of places that had bulletin boards and information centres, in hopes of finding the right place once again. I found myself at one of my regular spots, a new age bookstore. I struck up a conversation with a lady I had seen there many times before, but had never really spoken to. As it turned out her name was Katy, and the big surprise came when she told me that she was from Canada too. I couldn't believe it. As we talked we found out we had a lot in common. She also told me that a room was coming available in the house she lived in, and if I wanted it she would talk to the lady that owned the house about my moving in. Well I was so happy I could have kissed her. I said yes and in a matter of days I moved in with Katy.

The house I was now living in was in a direction completely opposite from where I had been. It was quite large with an ample back yard that was completely surrounded by a six foot cement fence. There was a lot of potted plants on the patio in the yard to add to the greenery. I knew immediately, I would be happy here. Katy was a wonderful lady, and the house had a good feel to it. So I settled in hoping that this would be my home for the length of my stay.

It wasn't hard getting used to the comfort of this home, and that was exactly what I felt here in this place. It was almost as if the whole world shut off once you closed the doors behind you. I am not sure what it was, perhaps the cement fence around the yard. or maybe it was the fact that the house was built in a slight depression so the street noise passed over the house. Whatever it was that allowed the sense of peace to exist in this place I was most grateful for it. A sense of peace was what I needed most now, there had been so much change and turmoil in my life, even the amount of mental processing I needed to do, that t felt as though I could sleep for a week. But there was still a fear in me of sleeping, at least deep sleep. I knew I was vulnerable when I slept and there seemed to be nothing I could do about it, but at the same time I could not hold off from sleeping and so I closed my eyes wondering where I would go once the dark blanket covered my mind.

Then when I opened my eyes I couldn't seem to focus on anything. It was almost as though I was in some kind of fog or a place where all shapes were indiscernible. running into one another. I felt the need to get up and move and though I couldn't see where I was going because everything looked the same no matter where I turned my eyes, a voice inside me just kept saying "Go forward". What choice did I have, I didn't know where I was, I was frightened and I didn't know how to get back to where I came from so the only direction I could go, was forward.

Sometimes it is not possible to know whether to trust the voices you hear in your head, but I did not feel I had a choice in this situation. So I placed one foot in front of the other and I went forward or at least what I thought was forward. I had only walked a few minutes and the fog seemed to be clearing. I could see I was entering a beautiful valley. It was then that I realized I must be sleeping. I felt a little less anxious now so I stopped to enjoy the gorgeous scenery in front of me. Off in the distance there were snow capped mountains, they had that blue haze that happens just below the snow line that created the illusion of blue rock. At the base of the mountains there were miles and miles of green meadows that were covered in wildflowers that were in full bloom, and all through this extended field there was a stone path that wove its way from where I was standing to the base of the mountain.

As I scanned the horizon I could see deer grazing in the grass at a distance from me. I felt as if I could spend the rest of my life here and never see another living soul. However once again I could hear that voice in my head telling me to press on. So I started to stroll down the rock pathway as slowly as I could just because I didn't want this feeling to end. After I had walked for awhile I was told to turn to the left, and there beside me was an opening. The opening had been carefully marked by a group of stones placed in a circular shape around the hole that led to somewhere below the surface.

I knew I had to enter the opening, but I did not know to where it led and there was only one way to find out. So into the hole I went. As soon as I entered the hole I felt the fear penetrate me once again as my body started to descend in a spiralling motion at an accelerating rate of speed. I seemed to be sliding down some kind of smooth tubular entrance. I hate being in situations where I don't know what waits for me at the other end of the line. Sliding downward seemed to last forever, then suddenly I could see light coming towards me from below. As the light came closer I think I stopped breathing in anticipation of what I would see or the pain that I might feel. I landed with a plop onto a stone floor, I remember thinking that should have hurt when I landed, but it didn't seem to.

I was in some kind of underground chamber. But the first thing I noticed was that the whole chamber seemed to be of green stone. The colours of green ranged anywhere from a dark emerald colour to light fresh spring growth green, but everything in this cave was green. I couldn't help the feeling that the stone itself was alive and somehow watching me. This I quickly dismissed as my own paranoia. As my eyes adjusted to the lighting, I could see that someone or something lived here. There was a table to my left with two benches on either side of it. The whole table and the benches were carved out of stone. Into the walls had been carved shelves and in some places there were intricate designs that I had no idea of what they were. On my right the fire made an amazing sight.

Flames rose from what seemed to be a fireplace, but there was no wood beneath the flames. As I walked towards the fire I could see that it burned in a spot that had been shaped to look like a long bathtub, and the way the ceiling curved, it had been designed not only for cooking but to heat the space I stood in as well. I bent over, leaned against the wall and looked up inside the fireplace towards the ceiling. I was looking for some kind of chimney, but there was not one to be seen. I had thought that I would have seen the smoke from the meadow if the fire was burning there. But the fact that there was no chimney explained that, however it didn't explain why there was no smell of smoke in this little green underground chamber.

As I stood there puzzling over the situation I felt the hairs on the back of my neck rising and I knew immediately that someone or something was now standing behind me watching my every move. There had to be some force that turned me around because I don't think I had the strength to do it on my own. All I could feel was my knees about to buckle. My body turned my head and then I was staring straight into the eyes of an old man. I am sure we both heard the sigh of relief that escaped my lips. Immediately I felt better, but also confused. So many times in my life old men had come to me in dreams to teach me or to push me forward.

"Well if I was young and handsome you wouldn't be able to get your mind off your hormones long enough to hear what I had to say, now would you!" His voice laughingly pierced the silence like church bells on Sunday morning. I was suddenly present again, instead of distracted by the mental mania in my head. "Ya, you're probably right", is what I thought, but out of my lips came, "Who are you?"

"Its all right you're scared and I know you're scared so the only person you are fooling is yourself. I brought you here for a reason so lets get to it shall we. Sit down, before you fall down, and listen to me. I am the old man who has been coming to you for years that is why I feel so familiar to you. The path you came here on felt like home because it is home for you, just not in your current time. How was the ride down anyway? I like to add a little drama to these visitations. it seems to be what you humans crave. You think an experience to be more valid if you exaggerate it. Some day you will discover the beauty in simplicity. You are going through many new and different experiences in your life right now. You have not yet learned to trust yourself as to what is real and what is an illusion. You fear that you will lose one world if you enter another. You don't quite understand the concept of being multidimensional. If I were to ask you if the world you are in right now is real or not, you would probably say no. But then your sensory perception would activate and argue with your logical mind. All your senses are activated here just as they are in your perception of the real world. You see, this world is just as real as the one you think you live in. The only difference is, you told your mind that this is not possible, so then you create the impression for yourself that this is your imagination and I am not real. But if I am not talking to you, who is? You are on the verge of breaking free from the mass consciousness agreement as to what the world looks like. All people do this when they raise their vibration."

"The way your physical eyes see the world is similar to the way the body perceives on an energetic level. So now you will not only start seeing as you always have in a physical manner, but, you will also see the energy of what is in front of you as well. You can expect this to progress to the point where some day you will be shocked to see how someone appears physically after you have seen their energy. You are starting to see all things as energy. Now you are wondering why I am telling you all this. This type of sight will be very important to you in dealing with the ones your people call Aliens. Your people rely all to much on their eyes for making decisions in life. They have disconnected their heart from their vision this is why they can no longer see how someone feels, and why they have lost the ability to be consciously telepathic. They cannot feel what someone else sees. There is no magic in being psychic, you simply have remembered to feel what is seen."

"The Aliens have a contract with you in this lifetime to help each other come to a point of understanding about the world you live in and how you create it. There is much to remember about time and space and how it functions. There is much they wish to share with you about this. However, to gain your attention you have requested drama. Humans have come to treat the television as a God. They give it the power to make decisions in their lives based on the information they get from it. Soon however they will come to realize that they are being programmed by the desires of those who wish to influence them. It continues to amaze me how people subconsciously consider television programs to be as solid and tangible as the actual piece of furniture sitting in front of them. Why do all these people think it is called programming? The Aliens know the way they are being publicized and what they would like most is for the truth to be known. This is part of the contract you have made with them. you have the delightful job of telling all those that will listen, the truth."

"Now it is very important that you let yourself learn to see in the new way we have talked about. In the times to come, there will be many Aliens, and not all will be to your benefit. But since the humans have based their lives on believing a lie. Many of the Aliens that promote the expansion of negative energy will appear to be positive because that is what you will be programmed to believe."

"You must learn to trust your newly discovered senses. That way you will not be deceived. You will also teach others to do this. Don't be afraid of these beings that come to you in the night. Understand that there are other forces on your earth that would do them harm because of their interaction with you. The reputation they have earned has been created by you the human, so take the time to hear their story, seek the truth in this and all things and then you cannot be harmed. You may be challenged because there are those that do not want the truth to be known, if it was, they would lose their control, and the people would have their lives back. Greed and fear attempts to ruin your planet and Mother Earth has had enough. The Greys have her blessing, she knows their truth and works with them. Seek them and find yourself. Work with them and find the future. Love them and you shall be one. Remember, every time someone's appearance frightens you because it is different from your perception of normal, you are only seeing with your eyes, you are not seeing with your heart. You idea of perfection only reflects what you feel is lacking inside of you. See with your heart and that is where truth is found."

With that he turned and walked back into the shadows, leaving me alone once again in unfamiliar surroundings. I blinked my eyes and kept them closed for a minute they felt very dry from the heat of the fire in the cave. I could feel the scratchiness coming out of them as the moisture replaced that feeling of burning. I slowly started to open them and as I did in front of me stood several pairs of grey feet. I could feel that panic feeling hit my stomach. I knew immediately I was on a ship. My mind couldn't conceive of how I could go from being underground one second to being somewhere in space the next. If I thought about it, I knew I would fall victim to disorientation. I knew I had to look up and deal with whatever was about to present itself. All I wanted to know was why don't we ever seem to get time to deal with one thing before we are thrust into another situation.

"When you have the time to deal with them, you also then have the chance to deny them or dismiss them as imagination. We do not have this time as a luxury." Don't any of the beings in my life talk with their mouths. As I lifted my head and examined this strange species in front of me. I realized that their mouths would not be too functional for talking as their mouth was just a tiny slit. There was something about these Greys that always felt so familiar to me. I stood there just staring at the strange and disproportional bodies that were in front of me, I don't know how long I probed them with my eyes but finally one of them approached me. I tried to step back but my legs wouldn't move. It came within a couple of feet and looked at me as though probing me with its mind. The skin was flawless. there was no enlarged pores or blemishes on the whole body. As I looked back into this things eyes, I felt very sorry for it for some reason, I almost wanted to cry, not for me, but for it and all things lost. I didn't know or have any understanding as to what it was that I was feeling all I knew was, it wasn't fear, but more like pity.

As soon as I recognized this fact somehow the fear faded and I became more curious than anything else. I felt like a little kid again. I wanted to poke and probe them just to see if they were real. If it hadn't of been for some sort of diplomatic courtesy I would have reached forward to feel their skin, and see if it felt as cold as it looked This time I was paying great attention to what I sensed in my own body. There seemed to be a curiosity with these beings too. I could see that they wanted to examine everything from a scientific point of view. They really did not understand the human being. They also thought of us as being very barbaric. They had their understanding of protocol, and wondered why I didn't know how they thought. It was then that one of them motioned to me to follow. Again I felt that rush of anxiety but I did notice that it was fading a little more every time it happened So with shaking knees I put one foot in front of the next and started to follow them down a narrow passageway.

We had been standing in what I guess could be called a holding room of some sort. Perhaps a greeting room would be more appropriate in my case. The hallway we were now moving through was narrow, white and almost luminescent. Even though it appeared to be darker in front of us, wherever we walked was well lit and easily manoeuvrable. We walked for maybe thirty seconds and then the hallway opened up into a large silver white room. This room was easily thirty feet in diameter, and as my eyes adjusted to the room being all one colour, it also looked as though it had an uneven surface.

As we moved towards the interior of the room I could see why I thought it was uneven. There was some form of furniture, but it didn't look like anything I was familiar with. Where the furniture appeared to be, was no more than a shadow, a shadow of shimmering energy. It looked like the waves you see rising from a car's hood on a hot day, but the waves were happening in groups or bunches. I was led into the room so that we followed a path that went in between these shimmering hues of white. I was beginning to feel as though I was in some kind of strange ballet where every move was planned and executed with exacting precision, albeit in slow motion. The way these creatures moved could have been like watching a willow tree as it blows in the wind, if they could have moved a little faster. As I observed them and the way they moved, it put me in mind of a society that forgot they had bodies. The greater part of their existence was in their mind.

I was placed directly in front of one of the smaller energy waves. The others fanned out to my right and left at forty-five degree angles. Then all of the beings seemed to be hearing something that I was not, they turned their heads in unison towards something that lay behind and beyond the empty space that lay between them. I could feel a high level of tension in the air, but it was probably just my own. These beings seemed to be completely non-reactionary. I think that is why they had such a cold look. After a few seconds that felt like an eternity, I could make out some kind of movement in the distance. Even now, I am not sure that I could actually see something at first, or if it was that I could feel a motion of some kind. Then the air seemed to ripple and another being like them appeared.

There was something different about this one though. To start with, I wanted to call this one he and when I did this, I realized it was the first one I had seen that I wanted to address by sex. He was also somewhat taller than his companions. The head seemed bigger and more heart shaped. But when he got within ten feet of me I could see what the real difference was. This one was old, how I know that I

60

can't really explain, his features didn't look wrinkled or sunken, but he had the presence of wisdom. Physically, he had what I thought must be some kind of mark of rank. Placed in the middle of his forehead was a clear white coloured jewel. It had somehow been sunken right into the skull, so it looked like it was a natural feature. As he approached the others bowed their heads slightly. I took this to be a gesture of acknowledgement of rank. There seemed to be no fear here, there seemed to be no emotion at all.

The one with the jewel in his head situated himself directly across from me and then lowered his body towards the shimmering energy just below him. As his body touched the energy field it transformed into a chair of sorts. It looked as though the chair had been made to fit his body specifically, it literally molded itself to his frame. As he was comfortably seated the others sat, and as they did, the shimmering energy fields below them repeated the transition to solid looking furniture. Each one of these beings looked so fragile, as if they would break in half if they bent the wrong way. All attention turned to me, as I heard the word "sit" in my head. I must admit to being a little nervous at sitting on thin air, even though I had just seen what happened with all the others. So I took a deep breath and lowered myself, all the time being prepared to end up on the floor and have these seemingly silent beings suddenly break out into horrendous laughter at what they made the human do. But that never happened, as my rear end hit the energy field, I could feel a slight tingle go through my body and before the rest of me sank into whatever this was, it turned into the most comfortable seat I have ever sat in. It was almost as if it was alive. I moved around trying to adjust myself and with every move I made, the chair would change slightly in its configuration to compensate for my new body posture. No matter how hard I tried, I couldn't get uncomfortable.

I had almost finished fidgeting, when I heard the voice in my head again. "I wish to communicate with you. Your people have called us the Greys. This is not who we are. We need to have some of you know the truth about us so that you may inform the others. We will not harm you in any way. All humans of your time seem to react greatly to physical stimulation. This reaction is a fascination for us. Are you ready to communicate with us?"

I hadn't realized it, but I guess I had dissociated myself from the situation. I had heard what the being had said to me, but I guess I didn't listen. Asking me the question brought my attention into focus once more. I went to open my mouth to reply yes, but as soon as I did I was already receiving a response to my reply.

"This is good. We have been interacting with you humans since your early seventeen hundreds. Many of you have been aboard our ships. we wish for you to be an ambassador between your world and ours. Many of you think that we are here to harm you. This is not a truth. We have come for your help. So many of your kind judge an action based on a visual reference. Because we look different, you see us as threatening. When you see us as threatening, we have no choice but to defend ourselves from that destructive energy. The only way we can do this is to create physically for you, the fear that you harbour. This way we allow you to indulge in your own fear without damaging our energies. You and your kind fear pain, usually of the physical kind. So many of you have learned to disconnect yourselves from your bodies, because you have suffered some kind of abuse. You are teaching yourselves to be totally sensory deprived. You are at the most critical decision point in the history of your planet. What you decide over the next few years, will decide the outcome of your species."

I knew all this stuff but hearing it from these beings, in this circumstance, somehow made it real. My brain also felt as though it was going into overload. My head felt like it was the size of those who sat in front of me. All I could think was "why me?" This was always my question, when I felt like I was in over my head I became a victim.

"Why you, will be explained later, do not confuse your thoughts with this. There is much to be told, before this is done. Of all of us sitting here, you feel a connection to me, and you do not know why. This as well, will be revealed. But first you must know why we are here. We are a dying race. We can no longer procreate. We have lost the memory for reproduction. I am the oldest among us, and I come the closest to retaining the memories. That is why you perceive me as male. In the beginning, it was our belief that by crossing time and space we could return to your time and use some of your DNA to reactivate our memories. So the necessary preparations were made and we came to this place. We had interaction with your people on a permission basis. We obtained the cells we needed and crossed them with our own They were placed in an accelerated growth chamber and carefully monitored. The cells were grown to be what you would call a fetus, then a baby and on into the stage of the child. Once the cells reach the stage that is known as seven years old we would once again cross the cells with our own and then place them back into our own bodies. Each child would be created male or female so that there was an equal balance of both so the chance of mutation would be lessened. We would then enter the growth chamber ourselves so that the cells could mature in our bodies. It didn't work in the beginning. But we were also aware that it can take many attempts to find the right formula. We discovered that the thing that separated us the most from the humans is emotion. We have forgotten what emotion is, and therefore we have no sensory perception in our physical bodies. There was a time in the late eighteen hundreds when your people started to deny us access to their cells. This did create a concern within our core group. It was then, that we as a people, separated. Most of us still work within the boundaries of Universal law. The small group that broke off were not willing to wait for the human to change their minds about access. The others knew that if they frightened the humans and then allowed the humans partial memory of the experience, it would create a large energy field full of people needing to add a drama to their life, and they were right. This was the first crash in your time 1947. This created a curiosity among the humans. They wanted to see the Aliens as we were called. The silence of your government increased the curiosity by vast amounts. Your people find great satisfaction in attempting to rebel against what they see as their controllers. The others were not expecting the amount of humans to call for an experience that did. They started to become careless, and more and more people started remembering parts of their encounters with us. The others did mass experiments and they targeted those that were vulnerable because of stresses in their lives. The more attention those on earth got because of their experience, the more you would call on us to offer you something different from your familiar lives. But along with an increasing number of encounters your race was also evolving at an accelerated rate. Your kind are extremely territorial and when that is challenged, violence seems to be the outcome. The more you shut yourselves down to experiencing one another the more you confine yourself to your own energy field. Your evolution is to move through the emotional part of yourselves. The only way you can experience your own emotions is to experience people in extreme conditions. However you are trying to confine yourself to yourself and so you chose a stagnation point. However you are not governed by your minds, you are activated by your souls and the soul only allows so much stagnation. So in an attempt to provoke you, a few strategically placed persons were allowed to follow their destiny, and the world went to war. The pain and suffering that was encountered on a worldwide scale was to try and bring to your attention what you are doing to yourselves by not allowing yourself to understand emotion on an individual or mass level. The wars mirrored what was going on, on the emotional level. You were killing your emotional level. Few seemed to recognize this."

The being suddenly stopped talking to me. I began to feel very restless and then my body got that feeling of all over tingling. The next thing I knew I was back in my bed and it was morning. I was in that space where you are not sure if you are awake or asleep, and my head felt awfully fuzzy. I tried to shake off what I was still trying to determine as a dream or not. But every time I closed my eyes all I could see was this jewel that had been in the forehead of this strange being. I rolled over to try and go to sleep, because I felt as though I had had none.

I must have fallen asleep at least for a little while, because the next thing I heard was Katy moving around getting ready for work. I managed to rouse myself enough to go out and see Katy. I told her that I had been on a ship and they were telling me the story of why they were here. Katy looked at me and seemed to be more concerned with the fact that I looked tired than the fact that I had just gotten off a spaceship full of Aliens. That had to be one of Katy's most powerful attributes. The fact that no matter what the circumstance was, she would always see the practical side. I didn't really feel like staying up, but I knew I would not go back to sleep now. I've never been very good at sleeping in the daytime. I can easily stay awake through the night, but when it comes to sleeping the following day, my eyes seem glued open. So as Katy headed off to work I headed for the coffee pot. It was sometimes difficult to drink to much coffee in Arizona.

The heat eventually got to you and all you wanted was to crawl inside someone's freezer. But every morning regardless of the temperature, that first coffee went down just fine.

I wasn't sure if I wanted to go into the Blue or not today, so much had happened last night, I didn't know if I could explain it all. So I went and took a shower and got dressed. Being from the north country, so many things in Arizona fascinated me. Towards the summer there, you never had to use the hot water the cold water was warm enough on its own to take a shower. Also the fact that they don't really have dusk or dawn. It is either daylight or dark. There may be twenty minutes transition time. Where I'm from, in the summer, there maybe lingering light for a couple of hours after the sun sets. But the one thing that is incomparable is the sunsets over the desert. That is one of the most breathtaking events I have ever been privileged to perceive.

Deciding to go to the Blue I poured myself into the car, and off I went to the other side of the city. On the drive in, I kept thinking of how fuzzy my head felt, I just dismissed it as being over tired, and swore to get more sleep tonight. As I arrived at the Blue I found that most of the regulars were out doing things that needed to be taken care of. So I hung around for awhile, almost grateful that I didn't have to talk about the experience I just had. I think I was still trying to decide whether I believed it or not. After a couple of hours I went home to take a nap, I just couldn't seem to stay awake.

The fuzziness hadn't left my head all day, so I just went straight to bed. I remember sitting staring out the patio doors and then I was asleep. It was only around six in the evening but I don't think even the mighty toothpicks could have held my eyelids open. I woke up with a start and looked at the clock I had been sleeping for nearly six hours. It was almost midnight. I had to get up and move around I have never liked just laying in bed unless I was sleeping or I was sick. I got up and read for awhile and then about one in the morning I became sleepy enough to return to bed I had no sooner turned off the light and I felt that sensation of tingling start from my toes and move through my body. My first reaction was fear, but then I thought about being afraid and wondered why I was. My previous experience on the ship had been intense, but not unpleasant. Then I remembered what the Alien had said that our experiences with them are formed by our own fears. So I tried letting go of as much of the irrational fear as I could. I wanted to see how they would appear to my physical eyes, if I didn't prejudge them as being ugly, because they are different.

So instead of fighting the all too familiar feeling, I allowed myself the enjoyment of it and went willingly. Once again I arrived in the large white room with shimmering furniture. There was only one being waiting for me this time however. This was the one with the jewel in his forehead. Somehow that didn't surprise me. Like he said during my last visit, I did feel very drawn to him in particular, but I didn't understand why. He motioned with his head the bow that I was now starting to interpret as some kind of formal greeting.

"You learn quickly, you have come to us without the fear you knew before. This is one of the reason's you were chosen to assist us with our communications to the people. Now come with me, there is much you must be told, and some things you must see to understand fully."

We left the large white room, and proceeded in another direction down a larger hallway. On the odd occasion we would pass another being that was some kind of crew member and they would bow their head in greeting. I try to be as observant as possible in all situations, and I was beginning to notice slight differences in the physical features of these strange beings. Some had a lighter colour to their skin. Some had a slightly different shape to their head. All I could think about then was how similar the differences were in humans. I was afraid of these beings because they were different, so then my fear had to turn to anger to protect myself from them. I kept thinking of how this was so closely related to the issues we have on earth of prejudice. I thought of how all peoples on earth have been segregated at times by those who deem themselves superior, and the only way they were really superior was in their quotient of fear. Their ratio was higher. The only time someone gets segregated by someone else is when the person doing the segregating is so insecure that they feel they need to create a whole race of physical clones. They cannot face their own demons so they project them onto anyone or anything they define as different.

"You are very right in that thought. Only those who are afraid can hate. If you can't feel Universal energy in yourself then you cannot see it in anyone else either. This we have learned at too late a time for us. I am taking you to the nurseries. This is where the children are. At the end of this hallway and inside the door you are going to see your own image."

At that point I stopped. I was by no means ready to hear what had just been said. I was afraid of what he meant by my own image. How could I have a child here? I knew I had been pregnant in my past but then I thought I had just had a miscarriage. The test had been positive but then a few days or a couple of weeks down the road, a doctor would tell me I wasn't pregnant. My heart began to pound so hard I could hear it in my ears. I didn't want to do this, but I couldn't stop now. Maybe he was right in saying that it would explain a lot of things. So we arrived at the door and as he stood in front of it, it faded into thin air and in front of me were several children, I don't even know how many. All I wanted to know was, where mine was. He led me over to the corner of the room where a little girl played silently. Her head was lowered as she focused on the game she was playing. As we arrived at her feet, she looked up and in her face I truly saw mine. She looked very much as I did when I was a child. Her eyes were bigger though and much more almond shaped. I carefully examined this child with my eyes and realized that she too was totally telepathic and could read my thoughts just as my host could. Her gaze met mine with the same intensity I could feel in my own. But there was something lacking. I guess I had expected some kind of recognition between the two of us, and their was none. Even though my logical mind said that was to be expected, my heart felt knew this child was not human. In my head I could feel the child thinking *Mother?' The word mother was a question not a desire, and then I realized that this child even though it was half me. it was also half them. This child had no emotion. They had no emotion. They had no concept of fear or pain or passion. They knew nothing of what life felt like. With that thought I was led out of the nursery and back to the larger room and requested to sit.

"We had hoped that by uniting parents with their children that there would be an emotional reaction. We have come to learn much about where our species went wrong, and we have learned this by watching you and your kind. It is true we have no emotion. That is why we appear to have no compassion to all those who feel they have been mistreated by us. They see us as being cruel and inhumane, however we have as little understanding of emotion as you do of the Oneness of Universal energy. We have now come to understand that our loss of emotion manifested itself into the loss of our reproductive organs. Your sexuality is fed by emotion when you are functioning properly. On earth now and in the resent past you as a mass consciousness decided to detach your sexual selves from your emotional selves. If you pay attention, you will notice it already happening to you. The female of your kind can't conceive at will anymore. The men are becoming impotent with greater frequency and at a younger age. You have taken the emotion out of sex. You now use it as a form if social statement or entertainment. When you are in puberty, you use it to make a statement about being mature. When you become adults you use it to manipulate others into doing your wishes or to punish yourselves. The males in particular have come to perceive sex as being love. Many would say mate with me if you love me. Instead of displaying emotional love it is safer for your kind to breed. Sexual union has become as insignificant as brushing your teeth. As you have noticed we have no teeth either."

I started to laugh almost hysterically, then I realized that they have no emotions so I guess he wasn't trying to be funny. Then I started to hope I didn't offend him. But with no emotions that wasn't possible either. So what I wanted to know was if he had no sexual organs why did I keep referring to it as him? And again my thought was answered

"I am one of the oldest ones here. I still have the memories of specific gender even though there are none physically present. I still carry the male energy and that is why you perceive me as such. You wish to know of the jewel in my forehead. Before we became as advanced as we are now, we came to understand that the natural world held all the answers to the Universe and to accelerated evolution. We as a species focused on the logical side of our beingness. We became thinkers and not doers. We wanted to go beyond the limits of the mind. So to do this a special crystal was developed that was designed to enhance the parts of our brain that are not normally in use. It activated our ability to become fully telepathic, telekinetic and also to create technology based on the electrical energy used by all natural elements. We started by working with these crystals outside of our bodies but we found over time that this could be enhanced greatly by the permanent insertion of a crystal within the skull itself. It developed into a mandatory law that all those born have the crystal placed in the forehead immediately. This did much to change our physical appearance. The amount of energy flow through the skull had so dramatically risen that many of our people died in an attempt to further science. It was then that we started to selectively breed the future generations. All those that functioned well with the crystal were bred with their equivalent in the opposite sex. The consequences were a progressively larger head size and a different head shape."

Even though I thought everything I was hearing felt like something out of a horror movie, it had an extremely familiar feeling to it. This sounds so much like something our own scientists would do if given the chance.

"And did."

That reply rang through my ears and reverberated in my brain. What was he trying to say, does he know our future? Does he know my future? There was that fear again as well as the vulnerability of being revealed. Then bang I woke up back in my bed sweating so furiously that I thought the water bed had sprung a leak. I felt like I wanted to vomit. My head was still ringing and it was daylight to top it all off. Life stinks at this moment. How am I ever supposed to go back to being normal now? How dare those Aliens enter my life and screw it all up? I didn't want to play this game anymore. All the rage I felt towards these Aliens was going to explode outwards any minute now and I was sure poor Katy would be scraping pieces of me off the walls for the next six months.

Chapter Five

Enough is enough. All I wanted at this point was for something to be normal in my life. It felt as though I had somehow crossed all these barriers from the world I once knew into this strange astral place, where you couldn't identify the players in the game. You couldn't even identify the game for that matter. The only thing that kept running through my mind was, why me? I guess I was unable to accept the fact that I had known these beings on some other level. Maybe I was afraid of never being able to return to a normal life.

All my life, all I wanted was to be capable of understanding the abilities I had and using them to the fullest. Somehow I don't think I was including the Alien interaction scenario in this desire. I just kept thinking that I was this tourist from Canada all I wanted was to experience something new, but not this different. Something a friend told me was on permanent replay in my head, "Be careful what you ask for, you just might get it."

Why is it, that, on a conscious level whenever we desire something we can't see the full ramifications of what we wish. I think we just see what we want to be the desired outcome and not the outcome that will actually be. The truth tends to lay within our karma and our core issues or our own self perceptions. Sometimes when we desire something, at least at a core or subconscious level, we don't believe we deserve it. So if we want something we don't deserve, I guess it will cause us all kinds of problems in acceptance and perhaps even in getting the goal. We tend to judge ourselves harsher than anyone else could, we definitely don't cut ourselves the same slack we allow our fellow man. So maybe I was just being to hard on myself. I thought that all this should just fall into place like changing jobs or something. But I guess this situation really is beyond the realm of my idea of a normal scenario. So I guess I should just let myself feel my panic, that may be the only way I can work myself out of it.

All this talking to myself made me feel as though I might just be going crazy. But in the long run all I wanted was just to have a normal life again Somehow the thought that I had never had a normal life to begin with never crossed my mind. How could I go home and even begin to tell people that I had been aboard space ships, with Aliens? It was then that I started to truly understand the control that the media had over the people. If it wasn't for all the bad press these beings had gotten over the past century, people may not have been so repulsed by the idea that they exist or that they are here on planet earth.

The more I stayed still and just thought the crazier I thought I was going. I needed to get out and not think for a while. Somehow even thinking that was funny. That was a whole new thought for me, not thinking, that was truly a challenge. I always run to the same place when I want to lose myself in silence, I run to the arms of mother natures loving care. So I headed for the desert. I just took the car and went into the middle of Sahuaro National Park. This park was set up to preserve the giant Sahuaro cactus. Finding my silence in the desert was my desired outcome, I only prayed it would be there waiting for me.

It was early evening when I arrived and the sun was starting to go down. There was still more than enough light to see clearly, but the strength of the day time sun had waned. I parked the car and got out to survey the land around me. I found a spot on the top of a little knoll, and sat down just to feel the earth beneath me. It was nice to know that something in my life was still solid. As I sat there I noticed the ants as they went about their duties. They seemed not to care that I was there in their midst. I wondered if I was an Alien to them? Did they know that I was no threat to them? Or was simply surviving, blinding them from anything else? Perhaps they just trusted in life enough to know that what would happen would happen and why get all stressed over it. Why couldn't we be more like the ants?

I opened my eyes to see the Alien I was now coming to think of as my friend standing solemnly in front of me. I knew they had no emotions, but I could have sworn there was a look of sadness in his eyes. Something that I was unaware of had changed. The space between us that had never been far enough away before, somehow now seemed too distant. I felt uneasy but without fear. I didn't understand what was going on, but I knew I soon would. It was in this moment that I truly came to know how love overcomes fear. I now acknowledged I had no fear of these people that I had come to accept into my life. Love transcends all pain and fear, and this I had integrated, now all I had to do was live by it. I closed my eyes again and we were back on his ship. I waited silently for the story to continue.

He nodded the familiar nod and then we sat down on the energy cushions. The air seemed filled with silence. Then as though there was nothing wrong he began. "You are at peace with us now. We needed for you to come to this point before you could accept what we must tell you. The people of your time still see things in terms of good and evil. Good is something that is desired and evil is something to be feared. This inaccuracy was not created by the one you know as Christ, but by those that would use him and his thoughts a saleable product. Christ was a channel for pure energy. He understood the concept of belief. Nothing was a threat for him because he had full memory of who he was as a soul. He knew nothing ever dies, it only changes form. It was in this knowledge that he was able to become the energy of life and death itself and perform the miracles that he did. For anything to be other than what it is, it first must die, even if in form only."

"As you eat, the form of your food dies to become the all important nutrients that feeds your bodies. To grow the food that you consume, the sun's energy must change form for the plants to be able to assimilate it. Therefore even the sun's life giving energy must die in a way. The only difference between life and death is the actual frequency that you are vibrating at. What appears to be death for one thing is life for another. There is no law of survival of the fittest, only a law of those more willing to change form. Our race are of those not willing to change form. It comes from centuries of conditioning in the belief that we are at the highest point of our evolution."

"With us the fight was always a logical one. Anything that was not practical and functional was to be eliminated Efficiency was our God It has taken us until this time to understand it is not about efficiency, it is not about logic, it is about love and acceptance. We have accepted that it is time for our race to change it's form of energy. There are still a few that deny this and continue the old ways, however they too, know it is futile. We have come for your help, for we cannot change form without you and your people. Without you it is impossible for us to free ourselves from this place we have chosen to be in. Just as you have come to accept us, we have come to accept the inevitable, we must die. Now I will tell you that which you have come to hear. This is the story of your history and of human's potential fate."

"We as a race are from your year 4055 AD. We have crossed the time space barriers and returned to you. The place we come from is known to you as the planet called Earth. Now I will give you a moment to deal with your reaction."

Earth!!! That's not possible. I'm from earth, and I don't look anything like them. My mind raced, trying to grasp at the straws that would erase those words I just heard. At this point I should have instantly started to dissociate, but I couldn't seem to escape this. Every time I get to the point where I don't think things can get any stranger, there it is right in my face. That's it I quit now. I don't want to play this game anymore. It's time to get off the merry go round and go home. My chest seemed to be tightening with every breath I took. Within seconds I felt as though I was going to have a heart attack. But that was not to be either. The being in front of me simply closed his eyes and I could feel his energy in my body easing my tension. It was a sensation like no other I have ever felt. It was as though I was suddenly completely empty and hollow. It was as though there was no emotional attachment to anything. It felt like nothing mattered or ever would again. Somehow everything had taken on the image of a formula. Almost as if everything was in numbers, stark and cold, with no warmth or aliveness.

But it did the trick and within seconds I was back to feeling a little more grounded and less like I was going to die from a state of anxiety. I am not sure if I couldn't fathom the idea that had just been exposed to me or if I simply didn't want to. Maybe I liked the idea that these were cold heartless beings here to terrify the masses for their own pleasure. I guess I didn't really want the responsibility of thinking that in some way I caused this, even if it was that far in the future. Every decision we make now creates our future, and in some ways I would be responsible. I didn't want to be guilty. As I thought about it though, I thought of the cave men and how they probably would have laughed if you told them that one day we would be typing thoughts into boxes, and sending the thought around the world. They probably would have gone into fear also. The longer I took just to calm down and think about what had been said the less obscene it sounded. Whether it was my imagination or logic talking, I could actually see how over time we held the potential to become as they were. I felt calm once again and I was ready to listen again. With that thought I could feel the pressure start to push against my forehead. I had come to understand this is what happened just before they were going to talk.

"You look at this from the right perspective. We may look very different than you do now, but we are your distant relatives. We share much the same DNA. The reason you have felt a connection to me is that I am of your direct line of descent. We are from the future but we still have rules to follow. When we return to gather the cells of your kind, we discovered that we could only mutate our cells with those in which we share a common bond That bond is in the bloodlines and the DNA itself. We had to trace our own individual lines of descent so that we could find who you would perceive as our families. You are my family. You are where all this started. Within each line of descent there was one person who held the key to our existence. One person who made the decision in their mind to become other than they were told they were. There were certain stress factors and karma that existed for you to make the decision to detach yourself from your emotions. In every family it was different. With some it was money, others had relationship problems, others just didn't have the energy to fight anymore. The people just decided over a period of time that life would be easier if they didn't have to feel it. One of the major indicators of this happening was the explosion of the computer age. People started to envy the computers, and they created programs in which they could play out the dramas in their lives. People became so intimately involved with their computers they activated programs with which they could fulfil their fantasies by accessing their visual screens. This was one of the biggest things that happened to create separation within the people."

"It was at this point that your future could have followed a purely technological path. The people were so distracted by entertaining themselves they were not paying attention to the genetic experiments that were going on in your time as much as they should have been. This time in your history was a mirror of the energy of Atlantis and the attempt to alter natural laws. It would seem that in many slowly evolving species, the desire to change the form is greater than the desire to understand the spirit. There was a massive movement in this time to genetically alter everything. Your foods and your animals. Everything became altered. It was the ultimate war on Earth. The scientists of your time decided that they could create a better ecosystem than the one that had already been established for billions of years. The more they experimented the more your world died."

"Natural selection no longer existed. The more species that were altered the more illness and disease started to spread. It reached a point where the mutations started happening naturally. Plants that had been genetically spliced with animal genes started to develop a new kind of intelligence. Animals that had been spliced with plant genes developed the ability to absorb nutrients from the sun. The boundaries between species slowly disappeared. What the scientists had started hundreds of years before, they were completely powerless to stop. The Earth was always more adaptive, than the humans that thought they could play God."

"So it was that the people could not adapt to the genetically modified species. Food was no longer food, but instead a sentient entity that was able to defend itself against the people wanting to consume it. Most of the population died off. It was then that an island in the middle of your Pacific ocean came out of the shadows and tried to save humanity."

"Unbeknownst to the greater population of your time, experiments had been going on with human beings. On a island in the middle of the ocean, underground laboratories were trying to create a super being by genetically splicing material from the most powerful beings on Earth to human genes. So many children were taken in this time. It was believed that aboriginal children in particular were closer to being a natural human so they were targeted more than most. When this became too noticeable, young woman from around the world started disappearing in mass amounts. They were kept as breeders and incubators for the genetic material. All the attempts to create a

76

new human failed. Whatever mutation survived the birthing process, did not last to adulthood, and so the experiments were almost abandoned. It is here that our two time lines cross."

"In our search to save our species we returned to the Earth in the late 1700's. Here it was easier to harvest DNA. People were more natural and less educated about the world around them. They were not so suspicious and were more controlled in their understanding of a higher power. Once again we repeated the process. This time our people did not die, but it did not have any effect on our attempt at gender regeneration either. When the energetics of the situation was examined it was found that the acceptance of technology was not yet inherent in the memories of these people. So we started the slow progression of moving very slowly through time in an attempt to access the appropriate time frame for regeneration. It was in this progress that we discovered others from our time frame that had set up habitation on earth."

"These others were not happy with our presence and attempted to destroy some of us. This event has come to be known to you as the Roswell crash in 1947. Some of our kind died in that crash and their bodies were kept for scientific exploration. As the others attempted to eliminate more and more of our kind, more accidents happened and your scientists developed a great deal of knowledge about us."

"When the scientists discovered they could not achieve the desired results in gene splicing using the natural plants and animals of earth, they turned their attention to Alien species that had been found over the centuries. They had the technology at that time to extract DNA from the skulls that had been retrieved from the ancient graves of those who died in the Atlantean wars. And so the experiments began. The crossing of the human being with humanoid species. As the experiments continued on the island, the Earth changed. Earth was returning to a wild state. The plant species dominated and their pollen would block out the suns rays for weeks. Animals became much smaller and the air was hard to breathe. Then one day a fire spread feeding on the accumulated plant material. First it spread across one continent and then a few years later another fire devastated another continent. It continued til most of the large land masses were bare. The only places spared of the great fire were some of the islands in the middle of the oceans. There were few remaining species of any kind."

"The experimentation on the island had successfully created what you would consider an Alien species, by splicing together the DNA from an ancient off world skull and the human being. They looked very much as we do now, however it was discovered that they could not speak as you do now. In the beginning the scientists did not think these beings were communicating with one another. The sounds they made were not language but rather a sequence of primitive grunts and screams. So it was assumed that even though these beings seemed healthy they did not have language or communication skills and therefore they would never survive long term. One day it was observed that many of the crystals that were used to store memory would vibrate when this new species were around. There were sounds that could be heard coming from the crystals the faster they vibrated. One of the scientists thought the pattern of the sounds was a form of language and when it was translated through certain frequency enhancers, it was discovered that thoughts were being sent through the crystals to communicate. So it was that translators were chosen and crystals were surgically implanted into the skull. Three of us were to speak for all of our kind. I was one of those three."

"The world was in a very dark place at this time, the human race was dwindling and the new species were being consistently grown in underground chambers. It was understood that before long, there would be no humans left and we would have to take care of our own race, and birth our descendants in the chamber. The humans taught us all they could before the last one died. Then we were on our own. Many generations passed. We were able to duplicate the chambers in colonies on the surface, but eventually our resources started to run out."

"At this point we knew we had to evolve we had to change and we didn't know how. In our desperation we started to do our own experiments with subtle memory that lay in the deepest regions of our brain. Memory that was not ours but came from the decoded DNA of our forefathers. It was then that we found the coding for space flight, and time travel. We took the resources that we had left and built a ship that could transport us through space and time. The first trips back in time were made to replenish resources and as we did that we built more ships. The more ships we had the more we could harvest and build ourselves up. Over time our numbers became strong and we became masters at harvesting our needs from other times."

"We should have payed closer attention to the solution that was used to grow bodies. As time passed it seemed that the beings that were birthed from the solution were not as strong and did not live as long. We came to the point of realization that so many lives being born from the solution, had drained the life force from it and we as a species were soon to become extinct. So we started to research how we were created and tried to use DNA to create a new species that could procreate. It didn't work. That is when we decided to try and harvest DNA from our own distant relatives in the past. We were all half human and half off world species. Our solution had dwindled in life force and we needed to use human females as initiators to start the process. This is how we came to be revealed. This has not worked and our species will not survive. The earth of your future is slowly recovering, and eventually a new species will relocate here. Our time, has passed."

I woke suddenly and sat upright only to feel like my body had been put though a meat grinder. Every inch of me ached. So I lay back down in my bed and just started to gently rock back and forth, as though I was trying to get some feeling back into my circulatory system. Katy must have heard me moving about because she burst into the room and looked at me as though she had seen a ghost.

"Are you all right? Where were you? Every time I checked on you all you were doing was sleeping. I was tempted to put a mirror under your nose to see if you were still breathing or not. I knew you were all right but I was worried, what if you didn't come back? I kept asking my guides if I should waken you and they just said no, that you were working and not to disturb you. That is all well and fine for one day, but three days is pushing the limit, even for me."

Three days I thought. How could I have been gone for three days? And why didn't I have to go to the bathroom? I guess that was kind of a strange concern considering I had just been in a place that most people would lock me up and throw away the key just for talking about. I guess it was about that time, that I realized that I had learned to exist in a world that most people would consider bizarre. I was starting to get some feeling back in my body now, and so I sat up on the edge of the bed I turned to Katy and hugged her knowing that she would always be part of my family and really feeling how much I loved her at that moment. I thought about trying to explain to her where I had been and what had happened, but when I opened my mouth to say something it was like my vocal chords weren't working. In that same second I heard a familiar vibration in my head saying that now was not the time. So I just assured her that everything was all right and that I was safe. The place where I had been was of no danger to me, and that I had learned a lot. I also thanked her for watching over me, like an angel I thought. I felt the necessity to inform her as well that, this would probably be part of an ongoing process with me for the rest of my stay here in Tucson. I explained that I was being taught the future history of the planet and the importance of the role that I am playing here on earth so that I can consciously assist in the fulfilment of my destiny. Katy being the loving and accepting soul that she was let it be at that and told me to come with her and we would get something to eat.

I think if it had of been me, the curiosity would have killed me not to know where I was but Katy knew better. So we went to the kitchen with a stop along the way in the bathroom just to make sure everything was still working properly. I was exhausted however. Even though my body was sleeping, my consciousness was awake and going through all that was being shown to me on an emotional level. The more I seemed to wake up, the more aware I became of being exhausted beyond the point of being coherent. I didn't even really have the energy to eat.

So I sipped on some soup and thought about where I had been. Katy had to leave for work in the mean time so I was all alone once again. I sat and thought about how I had gone through everything I had been told about. It was as though I was there and present even though it was in the future. I saw the events of the future in my head but it appeared to be in front of my eyes. Yet as I saw the pictures form before my eyes I could feel the emotional state of the mass consciousness of the people and the individual state that they were in at any given time in history. I wasn't so sure that I really liked this idea. This was far too emotional for me. I didn't really like emotion all that much. It was all fine and dandy to be happy or in love and I guess it was even fine to be sad or angry sometimes, but those emotions were nothing like the intensity that I felt when it came from the mass consciousness. I can't describe the depth or the power that this kind of emotion holds, or what it does to the psyche, when you dive into it. I think this is where words offer no validity of experience. There are so many things that go beyond words. The energy of an experience is the only state of reality in which one can experience the truth of the matter.

I was beginning to understand how the mind affected the body through the experiences that I had been involved in during the past few days. My physical body hadn't moved but I felt as though it had been through every action I had bore witness to. As a matter of reasonable deduction, I decided that even though the body doesn't literally experience things on a physical level, whatever the mind perceives to be, the body translates as being fact. This is why visualization is such a powerful tool for athletes. The cellular level of their bodies memory, sees action, even if it is through the minds eye, as needing an physical response.

So with everything that I had gone through in the last few days, my body interpreted it literally. In some ways I had been through a war. I decided it was time to go back to bed and sleep off some of the time travel intoxication I felt. So that is just what I did, I knew that I would not be interrupted again, at least not for a few days.

I had slept for twenty four hours when I woke again. This time I woke feeling as though I had slept only eight hours and without the previous body pain. I was quite refreshed and feeling pretty normal. I got dressed and ventured into the kitchen for a coffee and something to eat. Katy was up watching television, and made a comment about my not being a very good roommate, all in jest of course. With my coffee made I sat down beside her, and thought of telling her at least some of what had been happening to me. We first did the shop talk conversation of course. Katy was never one to push or pry if she thought I didn't want to talk. But after that was over, I said that I had been to the future and I didn't like what I had seen. Katy asked if we could change it. I replied with a yes and proceeded to say more about things that I hadn't really been aware of until that moment.

The first thing we must learn to do is feel. We have put a lot of distance between us and that feeling mode. We do not understand the importance of what feeling really is. The media has offered us no help by exploiting sex and violence. Seeing brutal acts of pain put upon the beings that we share this planet with had created a state of desensitization. We had forgotten the fine art of empathy. We have replaced the ecstasy of sensuality with the idea of sexuality and our concept of what that is. has become distorted. There is more foreplay involved in making dinner than there is in making love. We have taken the intimacy out of sex, and the emotion out of love. Even the love in sessions of the sixties got distorted. The right idea was there, but it was misunderstood as an act of physical gratification and rebelling against traditional roles, instead of gratifying the soul. Love and sex have become the same word for far too many people. Sex should be the physical manifestation of the emotion of love and when it is performed, it should be offered with love. It matters not who you are sexually involved with, as long as both people are consenting it is the act of loving that is so important. Orgasm should not be the goal, but rather part of the journey of the act of sexually manifested love.

This is part of the reason that so many women have developed the inability to orgasm. It is the orgasm itself that is the energy of creation in action. People have sex for themselves now, sometimes not even thinking of the needs of their partner. What is so misunderstood is the fact that just as much pleasure can be derived from fulfilling your partners needs as your own. If the body was treated as an adventure, then discovery is of the utmost importance. Discovery is necessary for understanding and therefore appreciation. and appreciation is a path that leads directly to love. So as we learn to discover the bodies of those we love, we should also learn to discover our own, for this will only lead to a greater understanding of the part of us that lives in others. All people are simply mirrors of our own inhibitions and fears and through understanding we will not only erase our own fears, but also the fears of others. People learn from example. not from being told.

So without first stopping to think why sex is so important in this society, people have gone about falling into the trap of acting it out instead off feeling it out. Sex is as integral to feeling and our evolution, as rain is to growth. Without emotion sex will become irrelevant and without sex we will not become fulfilled emotionally as human beings. It was almost difficult for me to think of how much my sex life would change now that I understood the importance of it. I no longer wanted to just have sex, I now wanted sex to mean something when I had it. And the only way it could mean something for me was if I was with someone I really cared about. That need to bond at a soul level with someone was strong with me now, and I knew it would happen some day, but for now I must be content to understand instead of explore.

Katy and I talked for quite awhile about my experiences. As I listened to myself talk I thought for sure that I would be thought of as crazy, but Katy took it all in and decided that I was right. She still wasn't positive about the Aliens but she did know something was going on and if it was Aliens, then she would accept that. Some of the things that I had seen in the last few weeks of my life had changed me forever. I knew there was no way that I could go back to a regular life now. But I still heard the words coming out of my mouth and I knew that if I was someone else, I wouldn't necessarily believe me. It sounded so much like an episode of the twilight zone, but I knew it was real, and I was quite sure that there were others out there that had been through similar experiences. And so after great thought I decided that I would speak my truth as I had experienced it, and let the chips fall where they may. I just kept thinking about Christ and how he spoke his truth and died for it. It must have been so hard for him to function as a human being when he knew he was not. But then again maybe he didn't consider himself human. Maybe Christ was an Alien. Perhaps he just took human form for the sake of the people. No, that's not right I thought. And as soon as I recognized that thought I could feel a familiar energy in my head once again.

"No, Christ was not an Alien. Christ was a consciousness. He was the culmination of three dimensional levels. At that point when he was present here on earth, people were once again at a transition point just as you are now. Christ volunteered to be born onto earth to provide an example of where it is that you as a mass consciousness can choose to go. He merged the third, fourth and fifth dimensional levels to prove to people that faith is really just about remembering who you are as a soul. He was trying to tell the people that they must trust themselves to make the right decisions in life, if they are to progress. However the people were not yet ready to take responsibility for their actions and so they made him a martyr. They merged their own perceptions of God with the example that Christ gave them. This is why in so many of your documents, God has extremely human like qualities. You as human beings put anything different above you. You actually like the idea of being enslaved by your ideals. Once you create a goal, you wouldn't dare change for fear that it would mean that you would lose the goal altogether. Christ was trying to show you that all things are within your command, and you have but to think and your thoughts shall create your reality on a physical level. If you believe that you can walk on water then, you shall change the molecular structure of the water so you can walk on it. All things will work with you instead of against you if you simply allow them to. All things have a consciousness and they are just a hologram of your thoughts. Christ had no fear of being human. In his mind it was a great honouring to be chosen to help create a new level of consciousness. The more that is learned of that time frame, the more that Christ ties into all religions. It has been said that he was with the Essenes and the Druids. There was even the possibility of being with the Buddhists. The consciousness of the Christed one was trying to say that all these belief systems are only a part of what he was. It is not that he was the only right one, but more accurately that we all have parts of these religions inherent within us. This is where the truth of religion is found. There is no single religion on your planet today that is the right one. Even if you mixed all religions into one it still would not be the whole truth. Mankind refuses to see from an inter dimensional level. Instead he looks only to his own small space in time for his reality."

"Fear confines you to not see the truth. Christ did not have that fear. He had full memory of who he was and knew of his own soul. Therefore the fear was non-existent. Even when he was being crucified it was only the perception of the people that he was in pain. This was the reflection of their own fears of pain. Christ knew no pain, for he was not in his body. The body can only feel pain when there is fear. The body becomes aware of danger and sends it to your brain as a signal, and that pain is your reflection of the fear of the impending danger. Pain is simply another form of stimulus and can be controlled at will. So I hope this has been of use to you and I hope this alleviates some of your guilt that Christ died on a cross for you. That is the religious interpretation of what happened, it is not the truth. What happened at that time is not necessarily accurately recorded just as the events in your current time are not accurately reported. Remember, the report of an event is always interpreted through the filters of the individual reporting it."

Katy looked at me as if to say "You're back now?" I hadn't realized it but I guess I had not been very present for the last few minutes of our conversation. As a matter of fact I had remembered nothing of what she said. So I quickly explained what had been going on in my head. I felt kind of disturbed at the moment. I guess I had started to accept the fact that they could communicate with me in the dream state, but I hadn't thought about them talking to me in my everyday waking state. I guess maybe it bothered me because I could still dismiss that fact of their existence as a dream if I really wanted to, but when I was fully awake, the only thing I could do was think that I was losing my mind. What he had said about my guilt of the crucifixion was none of his business. I could feel myself reacting because of a privacy breach. I didn't appreciate anyone telling me what I thought even at the best of times. So I proceeded to do some Alien bashing for awhile and then it dawned on me, if he knew what I was thinking just in my conversation to Katy when I was calm, he surely would be hearing what I was sending out now. My first thought was that I would be hurting them because I felt so volatile, but then my next thought was to question what was I afraid of. I was beginning to see the pattern of my reactions. These Aliens were right, all reactions were based in fear. So now I had to ask the question, what was I afraid of ?

Yes I was intensely private, but it was more than that, it was personal. I had a couple of days to think about it Time here was passing so quickly. It was almost as though there was no thought of time. Or perhaps I was just so involved in the thoughts that were passing through my mind I had lost time. A very good astrologer once told me that everyone's quest is to get off their chart. Perhaps it is every human's desire to go beyond time. I could honestly say I knew what it was to live in a timeless zone. Somehow there is no conscious concept of the hours that passed, there is only day and night, and even that all runs together. It was getting to the point where I was sleeping as I wanted to instead of confining my hours of sleep to the dark and being awake in the day. I would be awake half the night and sleep half the day,. The importance of this was that I followed the rhythms of my body without challenging them. I believe this gave me that sense of timelessness we all crave.

Our sense of time is heightened when we have to go against our bodies natural rhythms to live life. So I started to realize what it was like to be timeless, and I have to admit it was a feeling that I liked. Along with the loss of time, seemed to go the loss of pressure. The stress that is involved in everyday existence had disappeared along with my sense of time. After some perplexing questions about how the two would go hand in hand like this, I finally came to a conclusion Stress creates a boundary in life, it limits the soul and the energy field by compressing it into a space that is too small, so that it can't expand, and in essence it can't breath. Time does a very similar thing it creates a boundary for the mind. Have you ever noticed how many times. you can't do something because you don't have enough time. Therefore you set up boundaries for yourself, thinking you can't do what you want and then it just snowballs, into deprivation and then the feeling of being old, and that comes from not being free to do what you want. So stress and time are just more boundaries we use to add to the illusion that we create our world with. They keep us from going beyond being human. Even the words human being, is a form of constriction. It makes a statement that we are no more than human. Our state of being is human and there is no expansion on that.

It was at this point that I became crucially aware of the veils of time and space and how they were constantly moving and instead of merging were starting to move as sheets blowing in the wind. This was one of the major reasons people were losing their sense of balance, sometimes literally. When people lose their boundaries they don't know how to function, and that is when they become dependent. This is when they will turn to the powers that be for their guidance. This can be a dangerous moment in time.

When people turn over too much of the responsibility for their existence to a handful of people they are allowing the minds of a few to make decisions for the minds of many. This is how we have ended up with the state of confusion that we have. People that don't want to take responsibility for themselves based on Universal laws. So they deny their own power, give it away and allow someone else to use it. So on some level I was about to make a conscious decision to start using my own power to make my decisions based on the Universal laws that I was now learning I knew this would make the greatest change in my life that I had yet experienced. But I also knew it would bring me the greatest difficulties. Not everyone liked the idea of being unlimited, and so I would have a battle on my hands. There are far too many that like the idea of being controlled and manipulated, and if that is taken away from them they will have to consciously deal with their own karma. That is something they have been tying to avoid, so perhaps it is now our responsibility to help these people face their karma by accepting our own.

Chapter Six

Being responsible for our karma is a huge undertaking, especially when it is done consciously. It is not that it is so difficult to do, but it is acknowledging the fact that you are responsible for creating a reality that previously you blamed others for. Karma are the patterns that have crossed time and space to take root in our current lives. It is what our astrological charts are based on and even how our physical bodies are structured. Just as we can change the shape of our bodies with determination and will, so can our karma be eliminated. I knew I had some heavy karma to work through but I really wasn't fully aware of the extended reach it had into my life, and so it happened one day that a gentleman came to see me. Through the course of our association t found out that he was an astrologer. We decided to do an exchange of services. I am still so very thankful for this man Micheal. He did what no one else had been able to do up until that point. He made my whole life make sense. There had been so many incidences in my life that were just too bizarre for explanation. What it came down to was the fact that I really haven't been on earth too many times and the only times I do incarnate here is when earth is in the tremendous turmoil. He said that I carry what is called trans formative energy. It would seem, that if someone is looking for change in their life, they call me into it somehow. That change can happen in many ways. Some people have misinterpreted that for stirring up trouble, but that is a perception that is not exactly accurate. For me, this ability has created a lot of havoc in my life, especially in the form of speaking my truth and losing friends over it. What Micheal did for me, allowed me to understand this. He is an extraordinary person. Though he reads astrological charts formally, he is so much more than that. I believe that Micheal is a pure channel for higher knowledge. He knows a great deal about sacred geometry, and people, and how it is that they need to change their lives. Micheal is far beyond human already and that is why life is sometimes strange for him. I owe a lot to this man for helping me understand my life and the responsibilities that I need to own up to.

Power had always frightened me to a certain point. The fear that I would misuse it. It was through Michael that I came to understand that my mission in this life is to own that power again, with the knowledge that I won't abuse it. So Micheal came into my life and over the process of time, came to assume the position of wise counsel.

I knew the time was drawing near again that I would be with them, the human aliens. I felt as if I was never without them now. I could at any time think of them, ask a question and they would respond in my mind. Even though I was not on board the ship, at times it felt as if I were flying. The interaction with them had somehow made my connection with all things stronger and clearer. For me this was the perfect manifestation of the saying " It's not that seeing is believing, but believing is truly seeing." This was a reality for me now. As I allowed myself the comfort of belief, I did start to see once again as I had when I was a child. It most definitely brought a certain freedom that I hadn't experienced in years. It was as though the fear was fading and the veils were parting because I was no longer separating myself from the Universe. There were times when I would experience myself as a part of whatever I was looking at. If I saw the cactus I would suddenly feel myself in them. When I drew my attention to the birds or the animals all I could see was myself. The feeling was one of elation and of peace. The more I became a part of everything the more secure I felt. I was no longer alone. Not that I ever really had been alone, but that had been my how I felt. I wondered if these experiences I was having with oneness had anything to do with what the Aliens had in store for me next. It was funny, that at times I found myself almost missing these strange otherworldly relatives.

My body was becoming a highly sensitized piece of equipment. I could feel the vibration of the sun on my face. I could sense colours around people. I had gone from thinking about the truth to experiencing it. It is something you really cannot explain or describe, it is just something you know. It's like, you hear the phone ring and you automatically know who is on the other end. You can't explain how you knew, you just did. The communications I had with everything around me was no longer a conscious thought, it was now an instinct. It has always been my belief that when something becomes natural enough to be called instinct, this is when you bypass doubt. When you have to stop and think about something, you leave room in your mind for doubt. But when you simply react, based on a knowing that is buried deep inside, that is when you are experiencing the truth of your connectedness. I couldn't decide what all this new knowledge made me feel. At times it was overwhelming, but then again it had a sense of power to it. Power has always had an attraction, repulsion action on me. I would be attracted to places or people of power and then dislike what the power represented. It is only now that I am coming to discover that it is not the power that I dislike, but the abuse of power in the name of truth. Most people would think of power as the ability to control events outside yourself. At this point I was not sure that anything outside myself could be controlled.

There was so much to learn from these beings that I couldn't even begin to imagine where it would take me. I quite honestly felt very honoured to be chosen to participate in the re-education of the people. Although I can truthfully say now that I had no idea what kind of resistance I was up against. We are creatures of habit and do not like anyone who disturbs our habits. If we are actually forced to change our train of thought, we can get stubbornly vengeful. The typical reaction is to resist the point of the disturbance, until it stops disturbing us. This is why all through history it has usually taken a genius, a psychotic or a radical to make any real difference in the world. The only difference between the three is whatever common opinion is at the time.

I knew that within the next couple of days I would be called back to the ship to experience some of the final instalments of my educational process. I looked forward to them as much as I was hesitant. It was not that I was frightened anymore, but the fact that I didn't always have an easy time going through the process of seeing what we do to ourselves and this earth. Much of what I had gone through was not pleasant. And for all this understanding to be integrated, it seemed I had to go through it as a physical experience. So for all the pain and suffering that had become a part of earth over the centuries, I experienced it as though I was there, living it. There were times I felt as if I had aged three hundred years in a few seconds. So I was hoping that my next visit wouldn't be so harsh, even though I could understand the necessity of it. Nothing is ever truly real, until you go through the experience of it.

I didn't have long to wait, that night as I went to bed, the feeling of intense tingling started at my toes. At the same time I recognized my escort to assist my journey to the ship. In the blink of an eye I was on board. This time I was more than comfortable. I sat into the comfortable energy furniture and awaited my host. I had been there for a few minutes when I could feel him coming towards the room. It was as if he was greeting me on his approach as though there was no time to waste. I looked happily towards the hallway and I saw his shadow approaching. I was smiling in warm greeting as he entered the room. However with the first glance I had of him, my smile turned to concern. His looks had changed. He was older, more fragile and looked as though his life energy was leaving him. He moved at a slower pace than usual. His whole body had a hollowness to it. It was then that I could feel the anger start in me. This always happens to me i thought, I just get to know someone and then they leave me, or they die. I cant ever let myself love anyone because my heart will always get torn out when they leave. Now this Alien was doing it to me too. I started to feel sorry for myself immediately, before there was even an explanation offered.

"That is one of the bigger problems you humans must overcome. The thought that the self and others are different. If you are ever to come to oneness, you must acknowledge the self and others on an equal and equivalent basis. If you get caught up in self pity you can no longer see the others or the help they may offer you. You build a wall with self pity. You will let no one in but more importantly you can no longer get out. It is in self pity that you will die. Why is it that you are angry with me because you think I am dying? I do not fear death. It is only a transition. It is your illusion of ownership of me. Nothing can be owned. If you look closely you will see that it is your own fear of dying that is clouding your vision. You see how it is you will feel when you can no longer see me, and it causes you great distress. You are not really feeling how it is that I understand death. You only perceive your own feelings and then transpose them onto me. Do not create this illusion for yourself. The reality is that I welcome death. It will be a good transition for me because it means that I have completed my mission successfully and you have helped me to do that. It is because of you that I am able to die. For that I owe

92

you thanks. This means that you have made your choice for the future. I see that you are getting upset. you feel I am blaming you for my death, this is not the case. Again this is the illusion of your own guilt that betrays you. You feel that you have done something wrong bringing about death. This is the conditioning of your society. It is still perceived to be a bad thing. In my world because of our state of growth it is a good thing. You have done me a great honouring by allowing my death. The choice you have made is one of importance. You have chosen not to become me, and because of that it is impossible for me to exist. I am of your direct line of DNA. You are the one who was to make the choice for all your future children through time. That is why I came to you. I am only here now because of my will and your desire to learn that which you must know. As all of your people make their decisions over the next few years, we as a race will disappear."

"As each individual chooses the path of spirituality over technology we will cease to exist. All of us have followed our lineage to the one who makes the decision for the future. In many the outcome is still unknown. But there are more of us disappearing everyday as the choice is made. This is why we have chosen to stay here, aboard the ship. All we can do now is wait. You have released me from the constriction of time, for that I thank you. That is why the time is so important now for you to help us inform the people of their probable future. We are a dying race. that has already been decided, and it cannot be stopped. Before the year 2015, this is the most precious time, your world will split in its decision, and if this happens it will create massive destruction. The earth will always manifest your thoughts in a physical way."

"A split in thoughts creates a split in the surface, this you would call earthquakes. Look to the earth and her populations, if you want answers to what you call earth changes. The action the earth takes is always determined by the people that live on her. Your own home that you call the shield. People there are very solid and steadfast. They are like the rock they live on. They stand up to time. It will take a lot to move them if they do not want to move. However even as rocks they can stay in one place for too long, physically and emotionally. They do not want to progress. They shield themselves from life and from change. People that flood to your corner of the world will crave stability, and this will be the illusion that they create for themselves. It is your illusion that the shield you live upon is safe from earth changes. However the earth can change its surface in many ways. You may be subject to drought, flooding and severe storms. The whole of earth is accessible to disaster because it is the earth that is obliging us in the physical manifestation of our thoughts. There is more that you must take into consideration. What you call earth changes will not happen on a physical level alone. Much of what you will encounter will depend on what you are here trying to learn this time. If you are here to experience physical existence, then you will discover earth changes in a physical manner. This will include the earthquakes and tornadoes, for this is the physical reality of earth. But if you are here to discover the mental aspects of the soul then you will experience the oncoming changes as a mental stress load. You will be owned by technology, your life will seem to revolve around electronic gadgets, and your panic will come from the loss of communications that earth may choose to manifest. If you are learning about the emotional processing, then you shall be burdened with sensitivities that will run you, instead of you running them. You will be able to feel the pain of the planet, and in some cases simply staying alive will be the test. Not being consumed by your own emotions or the emotions of all others that you will feel is what you must master. And lastly if you are here learning to integrate the spiritual being of self, then you will have the experience of all of these ingredients combined in personalized formulas. Each one of these realms represents a different dimensional level and integrating your own soul on a spiritual level means you must combine all these elements and balance them. So, many of the things you will experience, will not be of earth as you know it. Many of these things will be on an energy level and from other dimensional time spaces. The difficulty for you will be in bringing all these things into the body and learning to trust the self, beyond all condemnation, from those who do not see as you do."

"All of these levels have their own degree of difficulty, neither one is more severe than the other. Since earth has existed in the third, fourth and fifth levels for many thousands of your years, bringing you to your present time, you will exist in the upper end of the fifth. You will know and experience many things that the people from the other levels can't yet comprehend, and so you will be subject to ridicule from those people, this is where trust and faith in yourself becomes important. If you can learn to trust your own knowing you will pass the test of your own karma, and ascend. If you deny your own trust, you risk the chance of descent into another time space. So remember to always trust yourself no matter what anyone or anything says, follow your intuition even if it takes you to what you think is a mistake."

"You have developed a concept of God that separates yourself from it. It has been your conditioning to think of yourself as lesser beings than anything you cannot physically perceive. It is however, only the veils that cover your eyes that prevents you from seeing any or all of these other beings. If you were truly lesser than us we would not have come to you for assistance. At this time humans are especially powerful in the scheme of things. All of the universe in this dimensional time space and others await your choice. It is only from the third dimension when beings become self aware that ascension can come. It is possible to return to lower vibrational levels, from higher levels but you cannot raise your vibrational level until you have accomplished your tasks. This is why so many are watching you now. Many have been stuck in one level for a long time and they desire to progress. It is only if earth at this point, makes the right decision, that all can grow or ascend. We, are what happens when you allow those in power to manipulate you with fear. Do not feed into the holograms that are placed in your evening news, and the papers that you read in the mornings."

"All of you have had the experience of seeing or reading something that you just can't believe. This is good, you should question what your media is feeding you. Much of your media is controlled and meticulously constructed to put fear in your hearts where love should live. Remember to fully engulf yourself in the physical senses, because their are many realms that have no sensation to them. It is well known that earth is a pleasurable place and heightened sensation is possible here. The angelic realm for instance, this is a realm of obedience. It is in this realm that you discover dedication and perseverance, this is the realm in which you exist to discover complete and unconditional love if you have not discovered it before. But on this level there is no physical sensation, no stimulation, and no understanding of self, There is only the needs of the many, no sense of self. Personal choice does not exist. It is here that you learn the lessons of not having choice. That is why many of what you would call angels are in truth Aliens. They do not have the same physical limitations that are your boundaries on earth, however they are not as complete as you the human being is either. You need to make the choice to reclaim your freedom."

"The decision to consciously create your world is a powerful one, and it is a privilege that you have, that most others do not. All dimensions play the games by different rules. This is why in many ways at this point in time, the decisions you make will affect reality up to the twenty first dimension. Beyond that level it is a completely different form of reality again. It is why there are many that walk on the face of your earth today that are here from beyond the twenty first dimension. They have volunteered to be with you so that you will have the opportunity to make a free will choice without being overly influenced by others who would negatively influence you. These beings look as normal humans do, but they are different in the way they think. The only way that they could be on your planet at this time was to pass through three, four or five lifetimes in the dimensional time frame that earth holds. Most of these beings have been major role players in transitional times. These are the beings that hold the consciousness of love for the planet. They are what your bible refers to as the 144,000. They exist as twelve thousand groups of twelve. They are all interlocked and intertwined, and they are placed all over earth's surface. For their own protection, many do not even realize who they are. The only way that they could obtain access to earth at this time was to buy access, by agreeing to take on the karma of someone that was to incarnate at this time. So many of these beings are having an incredibly hard time on earth because they are not well experienced in the three dimensional levels that earth functions in. They have not only had to learn how to operate the human body but, they have had to relearn what universal laws are in existence in third dimensional time space. The complication for them is to re-awaken to who they truly are so that they can help the human being change earth's time space continuum without first being recognized by those that would silence them. This is why some are so heavily guarded by non visible beings and have been completely veiled from themselves. Realizing who they are while still in a human body can be terrifying until the adjustment is made. It is in that time of readjusting that it is so dangerous for them, this is when they are vulnerable to being identified by the others that work for the energy of fear. If those beings identify them they can confuse them. If they confuse them they can use some of their energy for negative purposes. If they are terminated, these beings once again they have to wait to incarnate. These beings have an extremely high energy output that is connected to all things from all dimensional levels up to and beyond the twenty first. The use of this energy is valuable beyond comprehension to fear based life forms. Much of the experience of this energy has not been experienced by the human being and is unfamiliar, and so it is not questioned. This is where negativity has the advantage because you, the human, have not yet learned to question things that you perceive as beyond your comprehension. Remember, nothing is out of your control. All things no matter what level they are from, must abide by your rules. If you were to decide that you desired only love in your life and that nothing else was acceptable, then that is what you would create. It is only because you accept your own inner conflict of anger and violence that your world has become so ravaged and raped. Your world is only this way because this is what you feel you have done to yourself. Again this is the indication of loss of emotion in your kind. But most of all the desensitization has lead to a lack of compassion."

"Compassion for others is a reflection of love for the self. When you cannot feel your own pain, you cannot have compassion for another, and this is the life of denial. This is where our society lost control. We decided that emotion was irrelevant, and even a detriment to our progress. That is why we are now dying. Do not make this mistake in your time, change your minds now."

I awoke from my state of altered reality and lay there thinking about what I had just heard this being say. It was as though I no longer understood what was reality and what wasn't. So I decided right then and there to stop thinking in terms of what was real and what was not. I knew it was time to let go of the need to define physical reality from non-physical reality by thinking in terms of space. It was kind of like thinking about cooking dinner in the kitchen, or thinking about work as it is relative to the space you work in. I had to stop making a judgement on what was possible. That is what negative boundaries does, it is a judgement call on your limitations. I was slowly learning that we not only experience this dimensional space through our judgements on our own capabilities, but, we also understand other realities as a reflection of the judgements we hold against ourselves.

So many things were coming to light for me. As I became more aware I also came to understand my emotional state from an extreme point of view. When I felt sadness now, it was extreme sadness, but when I felt joy it to was the extreme version. The intensity of life had been turned up for me in some way. Perhaps it was simply a passion that was surfacing. A passion for life for the earth and for the universe and all creatures that live under it's skies. Maybe I was just starting to see myself as a reflection of all things. I know that as I came to understand other beings and their struggles I no longer felt as though earth was isolated. I was beginning to see what a powerful place it held in the sequence of time. I had a responsibility to do my part, even if I wasn't quite sure what that was yet. It made me feel good, that I, as an individual could do something to bring change in this world. I could honestly say that I looked at the world around me with different eyes than I had before I came to Arizona. It was as if everything glowed with love.

As I watched the evening news, I had nothing but compassion for those that considered themselves victims of crime. I thought, if only they would understand that they were in control of their lives, and nothing can be done to them if it is not required for their own evolution. We all have our karma and our issues to deal with, but that does not take us out of control at any time. Karma exists on all levels from personal to mass consciousness, and we personally have a role in all of it.

One of the biggest lessons I was learning right now was, there is no such thing as guilt. Guilt is a complete waste of energy. Earth is a freewill planet, and because of this, victimization is not a possibility. On this planet everyday, many people are killed seemingly, murdered. However none of us know if this is part of their karma, perhaps in some way, it is something they needed to experience to be able to evolve. No one truly knows the path of another. This is one of the reasons there are so many so-called miracles. When people escape or cheat death it is simply because they did not agree to die at that particular time. For those who believe in guilt, it is just a reflection of denying control over their own life. They do not wish to be responsible for their own actions so they fall into the role of victim. This can serve many purposes, on all levels. This allows them to experience the difference between being a victim or feeling their own power. It also allows for pity or sympathy which they may need to nurture themselves. Also in some cases it brings attention from the public eye, of how the role of victim lives in us all, and we must constantly be conscious to move into the role of understanding ourselves.

I had really lost all sense of time here in this place. This is due to the amount that has occurred at such a rapid pace. It was as though I was learning major lessons, or going through intense experiences everyday that I was in the desert. I knew the time to leave was approaching, but I did not want to go. I had come to love this place and the people that lived here. This was the closest to experiencing a place called home I had ever come to in my life. So the thought of returning to Canada was not really a pleasant one. But I could feel the pressure building up in my back that said "soon I would have to go". All my life I have had thoughts manifest themselves in my body, but I didn't understand that's what they were doing until just recently. It was when I realized, what happened to me in the dream state had a literal interpretation in my body that I started to question what was going on in my body. In the last few days I had been going through this strange vibration, almost as if my body were shaking internally and I couldn't stop it. I didn't understand it but I figured it was probably just another change of some sort. It was late in the day and I felt I had thought as much as I could for one day, besides that I was falling asleep on the couch, so I decided to go to bed and await the start of another day from a horizontal position.

"Greetings. Time has passed since we have seen one another. The mass consciousness on earth is changing at such a rapid pace right now that we are constantly having to readjust our ships stabilizers, so that we do not go crashing onto earth's surface. It is as if no one down there can make up their minds to go in a specific direction, and they are being ripped apart. In the last space of time since our meeting we have seen many rips in the space time continuum out here. You must be careful not to be in that spot when it tears, if you are you could spiral into eternity. Some of our people have disappeared through these and have not returned. One of the most dangerous spots right now is above your place known as California The people there literally live on the edge, they are torn between staying or leaving because of the desire to fulfil their wishes pushing against the reality of their lives. Most of these foretold misfortunes are scheduled to happen approximately in or around the year two thousand, according to the prophecies. But what these people do not understand is that they are creating the reality of the earthquake. With every year that passes their quakes get more and more severe. This they believe is the build up to the "big one" as it is known. In just a few days California is going to have another earthquake, and it will cause mass destruction. This shaking feeling you have been experiencing, is the earth preparing to tear apart its surface. This quake will be felt in your space of Arizona. This is because so many of the people of California have relocated into Arizona but they have forgotten to leave their fears behind, so these people are starting to create their reality even in another place. In essence the earthquakes are following them."

"This is why the scientists are always discovering new fault lines that they didn't know existed, in places they didn't expect to find them. Over the next few years as well, the weather patterns are going to change greatly. This has two major causes. One is that the powers that be are abusing the new technology that they now have access to. The high intensity radio waves that are being projected into the outer atmosphere are affecting earth's magnetic field. So, very simply what is happening is, that earth at times has the control of the weather patterns taken from her."

"There are some people in your time that understand what is happening but they feel powerless to stop it. The other reason your weather is to get out of hand is because of you the people. The weather for the most part is run by the mass consciousness, and their thoughts. So when the people can't make up their minds as to what direction they are going in the weather has the extremely difficult task of maintaining consistency. Most of the people on your planet, in your current time, are feeling guilty. All for different reasons, but they are still guilty. Guilt seeks punishment and punishment usually comes in the form of some kind of pain. So sad!! All the people

100

thinking in this way, earth has no choice but to oblige your request to destroy using the only weapon she has externally, that is the weather patterns."

"You the people control the world without really understanding it yet. The weather patterns are programmed in to the cellular memory of earth, just as your appearance is programmed into the memory of your body. But when you decide to change your appearance you also change the programmed memory of the cells. This is why visualization is such a powerful tool in accomplishing your goals. As you imagine, you create. This is what gives you the creative powers of dimensional reality. So always know that even in the creation of your own life, you also create your world around you, even in part the weather. Now we must discuss more about the earth's magnetic field. This magnetic field is very similar to your own energetic field. It is anchored and established in many of the famously known power spots around the sphere. It is also anchored in many virtually unknown spots as well. This magnetic field is intimately connected to your own magnetic fields which holds the memories of your lives in place in your mind. One of the most common complaints that is to occur over the next few years is that people will have trouble remembering. This is due greatly to the fact that the magnetic field is being interrupted by certain technologies that exist on this planet. So one of the goals for your people is to strengthen their own fields so that they will not have memory loss. Most of the people on your planet in your day and time feel that the powers that be do not waste their time believing in the prophecies, or the predictions of current day seers. This is not true at all. Those same powers work with some of the most powerful seers and use them to guide their movements through time."

"It is well known that the earth is gearing up to shift, although the exact time is not known. It is also known that when the magnetic shield of earth, comes down during the shift, the people will lose their memories if they are not prepared. If those in power could create a false magnetic shield based on a slightly different vibration when the people recovered their memories, they would be in complete control, and the people would know no difference. So currently their is a race happening on earth for different ways to find the right vibrational frequency to take over the minds of the people when earth's shield goes down."

"What the ruling powers don't realize is that they are selling themselves out in the process. Those in power forget that just as they deceive the people with not letting them know the truth of what is occurring in their own countries, there are those that that are deceiving them as well. Unfortunately they have developed the attitude of being invincible. However they too are subject to deception at this point in time. So my message for you at this time is to develop your understanding and your knowing to a point that your vibrational frequency is beyond that of earth's and then none of this magnetic field manipulation can harm you. It is also necessary for you to join the others on the surface that are strengthening their own personal fields so that when earth's field falls, they can join their minds together and set up a grid system of love across the planet. This is what will truly choose earth's new direction in time."

"So as you can see there is a false race to change the direction the people are going in. This is where the actual tear in space is coming from. Understand as well that those in power will not be content to let this be a healthy competition in the history of time. No, they will have their assistants try to stop you in any way that they can . But the most powerful way for them to achieve this goal is to take you from a space of love and place you into a space of fear. It is in this way that they can also access your power and use it for their own goals. The most effective way to place people in a space of fear is by targeting them, or making them feel separate from all that they know. One of quickest ways of making people feel separate is to help a person feel as though every thought they have is not real. But it is very important that you remember everything that is done now is done on an energy level. They do have this technology now, even though the people are not aware of it. If the people knew of it they could counteract it and then it would cease to be a weapon. Technology can be bought from a wide variety of places depending on the price you are willing to pay. So as you feel things are happening to you but you cannot validate them, or perhaps your physical senses cannot rationalize them, you may begin to feel as though you are crazy. It is at this time that you will stop and talk to someone else to try and validate what you are feeling. This person you have confided in will most likely tell you that you are crazy, because this person is not a target."

"You must remember that the person who is a target will go through their life experience very differently then those who are not. Do not forget this. Do not expect anyone to understand how you experience your life. With this new technology, targeting is an individual experience, because it works within your own energy field. What you experience, another person may not even be able to feel. Those who are here volunteering to help earth and the people on earth through this shift are in the greatest danger of being targeted, because they are of the greatest threat to the controllers of the planet. That is why so many of them are heavily veiled until it is time for them to go public in their own personal way. As this new technology scans the earth to find these beings, it will pick up no abnormalities in their vibrational field, that way they can learn to defend themselves before they become vulnerable. These beings are in your current time in the numbers of 144,000. Where there is one there will always be eleven more. It is these groups that anchor in the magnetic field of earth in the times to come. If these beings can be eliminated then earth's control by the dark forces is assured Some of these people are being eliminated before they are even fully activated because they did not learn to trust themselves."

"This is one of the most important things that you have to ingrain in yourself so deeply that it cannot be erased. You must learn to trust that which you see and feel beyond the judgement of all others, even those that you may have considered within your circle of closest friends. We can see the tear happening in your dimensional space, you can only feel it. It is now that you are training yourself to go beyond the physical senses that you have relied so heavily upon in the last several thousand years. This is the only way you shall survive. All that is physical can now be replaced by holograms, and if you buy into it, you will be come part of the hologram and that will be your illusion. Lift your expectations and close your physical eyes, it is your inner eyes that see true now. Trust your own heart as to what is truly happening in the world, do not always believe the media for they do not always have the real story and all things that are publicized are first filtered through the structure that can deny their existence. On a consciousness level it is a free will planet, on a physical level there is no such thing as freedom on your planet currently. You must consciously choose freedom before you will have it. But for your kind, freedom is still coated with the fear of accepting too much responsibility. Freedom is not a physical state as you think it is, freedom is a state of accumulated knowledge, what you choose to do with that knowledge will determine your level of freedom."

"This is the state that you are currently growing into, and you can expect the rate of growth to grow in intensity into the year 2012. This is your draw line on the decision you will make. There is very little leeway as to the amount of time that this can be extended. There are many things planned by the dark forces in the first years of the new century. These things will only happen if you have not locked in your decision. It is time now to move towards your decision, and activate your conscious memory of who you are. I will now leave you as I can feel your emotions are going into overload. We will meet again soon."

All of this stuff was just going beyond my conscious ability to understand. It was as though I felt that I should understand but I couldn't, it all lay just below the surface. But when it came right down to it, I couldn't consciously remember. I was somehow looking through a glass plate at what I wanted without knowing that I couldn't grasp it without first removing the clear obstacle. It was so frustrating. I was trying so hard to be what these beings thought I was. I felt as though I was failing miserably.

As I lay there waiting for morning to arrive, I found myself wondering how the tear in dimensional reality would affect each individual's energy field. We are all so connected to the universal actions and reactions I was curious, as well as a little concerned, as to how this action would manifest itself. Perhaps this was the beginning of the separation of the worlds as we know it now. I was remembering a vision I had many years ago. The world appeared in front of my eyes as it looks now when viewed from outer space. As I watched it turn it seemed as though there was a fog or a mist being expelled from it and gathering in thickness around the rotating globe. After a few seconds of this I saw what appeared to be souls of people coming off the earth and disappearing into the mist. As the mist increased in density with the filling up of souls, the mass that was being created seemed to be forming a solid mass. As this mass became more solid it started to move very slowly away from earth. It was as though one bubble had formed inside of another and with the application of pressure it was slowly starting to move the one bubble to be vastly extended around the interior bubble. The farther the mist moved out of earth's atmosphere the more solid a mass it became. Also the farther it moved, the faster it moved. It looked just as though the souls of the people were creating this new earth, and then pushing away from the old earth. The last thing that the vision showed me was that there were actually two earth's, one was a solid hard core in the centre, and the other one was semi-solid, and in a way it watched over the other earth.

In the explanation for this vision, this is what I learned, all those who had made their decision to go beyond human had transported themselves to the new earth. This new earth is still in association with the old earth but is of a higher dimensional level. In other words it has become a form of parallel dimension. The beings of the new earth acted as teachers and assistants to the old earth, for they had developed the ability to transport themselves from one reality to another. These people had volunteered to help the old earth go through its transitions, and show those who did not wish to grow, a new way of life.

This is very similar to the legends of the gods in Greek mythology. These so called powerful beings were somehow bound to humans but did not live amongst them. In my opinion these beings created the mold for the twelve different personality types that exist on the planet today. I see it as being very similar to a tarot deck.

There are seventy eight cards in a tarot deck. These are broken down into two major groups called arcana. The major arcana is based on Universal laws and the spiritual qualities that exist in the realm of the human being. So all truths that can be incarnated into this current dimensional reality are contained in the major arcana. The rules of Universal law are also contained within this section of cards for this and other dimensional realities. Each one of these card are like a key to a higher knowledge, and if they are worked with, they shall be understood.

The other segment of the deck is called the minor arcana. This section of the deck deals with basic personality types and the ensuing karma that is created by the individual, allowing for emotional reaction. This is where most people are on their individual totem pole of development. When you shuffle a tarot deck and choose your cards, what you are doing is telling the mythological story of your present existence in this time space reality. But the cards can be worked with to see the trajectory of your movements on a physical, mental emotional and spiritual level. It is in this way that the cards become of great assistance in helping you to consciously decide the direction of your future. Reading tarot is a very simple thing to do, but you must first be able to see the truth of your own personal existence. Once this has been accomplished you are in conscious control or your life, and your path. This as I was beginning to realize was the place that these Aliens were in right now. It seemed as though all the levels of dimensional reality were waiting for earth to realize this, and to activate their own knowing.

Perhaps this is why earth is such a battle ground for control in the time space continuum at this point. Earth is playing the role of the post that holds the hands of the clock and allows them to turn freely and evenly. If fear and anger gain control, chaos will reign freely throughout all dimensional realities up to the twenty first. If love wins, all will have the opportunity to progress and leave their past behind them.

I was beginning to understand the power of the position that earth held and the reason for the 144,000 being present, here at this time. But along with my understanding was a growing feeling of being overwhelmed. I have always taken my responsibilities to literally. If these Aliens were targeting me to be some kind of a communicator, I wasn't sure that I could live up to their expectations. It was at that point that I became truly scared of who I was for the first time. It was within those few seconds that I felt a huge expansion of being mixed with my human emotions. Self doubt and soul doubt poured into every cell of my being. I wanted to run but had no where to run to. I knew I had opened a door way of some kind and there was no turning back now. But now I wasn't sure if I wanted the job that had been offered to me. I can remember thinking when I was a child that I was meant for a specific purpose. Even as a child I don't think I could have imagined this. The people back home had a hard enough time accepting me now, what were they going to do when I started talking to them about Aliens and changing the consciousness on the planet because if we don't those that are in control will do it for us and then we shall all be in a place of despair.

There went my imagination I was gone, off in one of my rides through delirium. I don't think more than five minutes had elapsed, and I was in a state of complete and total paranoia. Then it happened, I found out just how quickly you can create your reality. It was broad daylight out and all of a sudden in front of me stood three of the biggest, scariest things I had ever seen. They were powerful and the expressions on their face said, negative intent. I couldn't breath and I knew for a certainty that death was close.

The one that was in front started towards me and I was completely frozen, unable to move. I squeezed my eyes closed and waited to die. But after a couple of seconds it hadn't happened and I wondered why. I didn't like the idea of opening my eyes to see those big ugly things again but there was no other way I could see my impending death. I forced one eye open and then the other to see my attackers trapped within a beam of white light. This time it was them that couldn't move and they looked pretty panicky. As I followed the beam to its source, I was surprised to see my friend the Alien was projecting some kind of beam from the crystal in his forehead. I started to breath again, realizing that I wasn't going to die, and with that there was a strange and offensive smell and the bad guys dispersed into emptiness. I turned to my friend and thanked him. In response he offered me an explanation.

"They used to be in association with us, until we came to understand that the pursuit of our existence through force is not logical. These beings that were attempting to terminate you, see you as a threat to their existence. You have now become unveiled. You no longer have your protective covering that you entered into this world with. Now it is for you to consciously create it yourself, using your own energy field along with the energy that is available to you from the universe. Who these beings are isn't as important as you would like it to be. All you humans seek to label energies. Perhaps you should start thinking in the terms of love and fear and then you will have your truths and your answers. These beings will seek you out many times. Know that you can conquer them at all times. However you must battle them with love, for if you fall prey to fear, you fall prey to them. The more you fear the stronger they will become. It will be your natural reaction to fight back, but you shall discover this is futile. They can access you in the waking state or in the dream state. One of their specialities is to wait until you have left your body while in the dream state, and then go in and try to capture you within an energy harness. With this harness they can drain your energies to the point where you become vulnerable. Beware of them, but don't be afraid of them. They can see who you are on an energy level and they know you are here to help earth make her shift on the level of love, and so they will try and stop you. This is why it is so important now that you use all your senses and trust your knowing. These beings are technologically based, and they can affect a wide variety of areas. Do not fall into their trap and become afraid. If anything feels suspicious to you, it probably is. Trust yourself, you have now proclaimed yourself a warrior in the fight for peace and love. Trust yourself above all and you shall be safe. I shall assist you when I can, but eventually you shall surpass my energetic level and my assistance will be of no use to you. We do not have enough power left to be effective. This is why we ask for your assistance in this manor. I am here to help you, but you are stronger than us, so you must carry out this task."

And with that he was gone again, but this time I felt he went further away. I just started to shake and cry. I couldn't control everything I was feeling at that moment and the only thing I knew to do was cry. I don't know how long I cried but it seemed to me, it lasted forever. Every doubt you can imagine ran through my mind. I felt naked without my protective covering. But I hadn't even noticed it was there until it was gone. It was as though every eye in the universe was suddenly inspecting me, and I was there to stand naked before all of them. My body ached with fear and I was almost wishing those things had killed me. At least then I wouldn't have to feel this way, or have to think about dealing with those things again. I wasn't strong enough to do this. I had no training or skills. I didn't have a clue as to what I was doing. And trust? How can you trust yourself when you don't even know who you are? Eventually I cried myself to sleep almost hoping that they would come and get me, so then I didn't have to wake up. But that did not happen, and in a few hours I awoke with sore eyes from crying and my body still aching with fear.

Chapter Seven

All my mind could think of was "How could I have ended up in this position." This is not what I had planned. I realized I had a purpose, but I had no understanding of what that might be. For as much as I had been training myself to release my fear, I guess I had only thought of the fears that are encountered here on earth. I hadn't thought of including multidimensional beings in my list of fears. For as much as I had involved myself in the world of Aliens, I had come to think there was only one kind, not several different races. It is funny how we limit our minds to think in one way, and one way only. Expanding my horizons had taken on a whole new context. Perhaps that is what it really means to go beyond human. To go beyond our own limiting thoughts as they pertain to just this earth. We are, but merely, a small thin layer in this giant universal onion. A single cell in a multi-dimensional body. In my perception, since I have engulfed myself in what we consider to be spirituality, I have been under the illusion that somehow when we ascend there is no more tests and trials. I guess it's that old thought of going to heaven that still lingers in my mind. The thought of being constantly at peace after having dealt with all your issues being able to feel nothing but love. I was beginning to see that this may not be the way it really is. Maybe we have issues to deal with no matter what level we are on. However that thought was not nearly as pleasurable as thinking we have no harsh learning to do once we pass on. Maybe, I was just lazy, and I wanted to take a soul holiday.

The thought of having to deal with my fears of fighting something that I cannot see was about to become a reality. How could I battle something that was not really in front of me? What am I supposed to do, punch the air and hope I make contact? I guess it was at that point that I really made the decision whether or not I was going to go in this direction or not. We are all given a specific event or decision in our lives that will be the turning point, and start us solidly on that path. Sometimes the thought may not even be a profound one. It is just as simple as a fork in the tree, the only one that knows why the fork is there, is the tree. The more I asked why this was happening to me, the more irrelevant it seemed to be. It was becoming less of a self pity issue and more of how I was going to deal with this. The more I moved away from the why of it, the more I realized life would be so much simpler if we removed "why" from our vocabulary. My understanding was, "why" becomes a self pity word when applied to your fears. By the time you ask why, you have already made your decision on any given event, so at that point it is better to focus your energies on how to deal with it than to wallow in it.

By taking responsibility for any given situation in our lives, it allows us to deal with it so much more effectively. That in itself gives us a head start. So much was racing through my mind right now. If these things whatever they are were starting to bother me, they would have bothered many others as well. As I let my mind wander I started to view some of the events in history through my minds eye. I could see everything from the Lemurian and Atlantean societies, to the memorable Dark Ages with knights and dragons. Some of the others that came to mind were the discovering and claiming of new worlds by explorers, and of course the witch burnings. right up to the first and second world wars. It seemed to me that all through history these memories were actually mass consciousness decision points as opposed to simply historical events. But in this last century, there have been so many shifts in consciousness it has created chaos. We have advanced more in the last hundred years than in all of history. For me personally, this is mind boggling. This much change in such a short space of time does not allow for too much adjustment or integration. This puts a lot of pressure on us personally and at a mass consciousness level.

So the effect you get is one of pushing and pulling. A world split in half and both sides arguing they are right. Those that agree to argue may total five percent of the actual population, then there are all the rest that have not made up their minds yet. These are the people that are sitting back waiting to see who comes out as winner and they will join that team. Unfortunately it is not possible to do that at this time. We are at the extreme transitional point and it is up to each individual to make up their own mind on a personal level. We all have this decision to make and then we must be ready to stand behind it to become our true natures. Whether this be the stance of the warrior, or a communicator, a scientist, or a teacher. Whatever your true nature is this time, this is the stance you will have to make. And there are many of us that are nervous about being revealed. But as each one of us makes our individual decision it creates an cumulative effect that will lead to a fifty three percent mass consciousness decision. This is how the new world will be created. So the longer we procrastinate in making our own individual decision, the longer and more confused this planet becomes. This is comparative to the acid, alkaline process of digestion. If you were to eat all your acid foods together, or your alkaline foods together, there would be no problems. But on this earth right now we are doing the equivalent of combing our acid and our alkaline and we have a lot of indigestion.

When the indigestion of our population is discovered by other dimensional beings we add another factor to our existence. Those who wish to prey on our disharmony will come and place themselves in the most discreet but most powerful place to serve their purpose. This will usually be within a structure that is already hidden but powerful. These structures we are familiar with and label them religion, government and technology. It is within these structures, that most of the changes occur when we feel we have no control over them. What is really going on is very different than what we are allowed to know about. There was so much so fast, I suddenly felt like I was in many countries around the world, in secret places and seeing silent events that the public knows nothing of, so much that I couldn't comprehend all of what I was seeing. The next thing I knew everything went dark and a few hours later I woke up completely exhausted with no memory of where I had been or what had occurred. All I did know was that I had somehow tapped into a consciousness that was exclusive to the hidden powers of the world.

It appeared as though, those we see as heads of state and religious leaders of the world, are not really the ones that are in power. This confused me though. I had always thought of presidents and prime ministers as being the highest level one could go in this physical existence. Too much was going on in my mind, everything that I had come too understand was starting to come apart. The way I understood the world to function was all an illusion, but I still couldn't see the way it really functions either. I suddenly felt as though I had no structure. No boundaries to measure this world that I live in. It would have been easy at that point to just disappear It was the first time I had truly experienced the fear that comes with having all of your known limits removed from the structure of your mind. I suddenly understood that I am not separate from anything. I was part of the process and I hadn't realized it before now. The part of you that goes into fear, is the part you recognize when you see all the negative actions that exist. Just as you help create any of the good that occurs on this planet, you also helped create the pain and frustration.

No limits and no boundaries and not knowing the truth was not a comfortable position to be in. I hadn't asked for this, but now I needed to know the significance of it, why was I the being offered this information, and how many others knew of this? Time was running out and this was an immediate need. I knew I had to talk to my future self, to see the whole picture of what had just happened. And then I realized, I had stopped thinking of these Aliens as foreign, and I had started to think of them as part of myself, for me that was comforting.

"We have been waiting for you to reach this point in your understanding of yourself. You have started to experience the knowing you will need to survive the coming times. What you have seen, even though you may not remember at this point will return to you when you need to see it. The goal for all of your people is to go beyond being human in their heart now, you have activated the process of what you know as ascension. This process takes a different amount of time for different people. In most of your texts, you refer to ascension as something in which you shall leave your body and perhaps not return. This is not necessarily true. There are many types of ascension. In those who chose to leave the planet, they may attain this great knowledge, and then go on to becoming your idea of angels or guardians or even something else. But there are many who leave this planet that will not have the knowledge you seek and shall return at some point in time whether it be future or past. All of time travels in waves and any time frame can be accessed if you find the access point to enter physical reality. That is why you don't automatically go into the future every time you incarnate. You can go into the past as well. This is one reason the past as it is written, is always changing. As we take newly conditioned attitudes from the present and return to the past with them we can consciously change the memory of events.

There are some beings currently on earth that have only travelled through two or three different time frames and they keep traversing them continuously to try and help people change their karma."

"One of the reasons ascension feels as though it is an event that happens powerfully and in an instant, is that you may not notice all of the preparatory work that goes on in the body at all levels prior to the actual event. For you individually now, there will be many changes for you to face. These changes will occur physically as well as mentally, emotionally and spiritually. Of course one of the biggest changes you will see is an erratic pattern in your eating habits and your sleeping habits. You will no longer be able to predictably know what you want to eat in advance. You may develop cravings like a woman who is pregnant. One of the reasons for this is that, earths natural nutrients have been almost eliminated from her soils, you as a race have not yet learned to energize your food to meet the needs of your bodies. So for you to gain the proper nutrition to help your body function through the tremendous amounts of stress that it will bear, some of your food combinations may not make sense to you. What will happen is, a specific chemical reaction will occur in the body, provoked by the unusual combination of food and the body will provide itself with what it needs. This is one of the most important reason to follow your cravings. You may also find that eventually in your progress, you will limit the variety of food that you eat. As it is discovered what works for you personally, you shall refine your diet to as little as five or six different items and eat those items as the basis of your food intake. Many of you as well, will have to return to the seas and oceans for your answers to your cravings. A clue for the individual to help them figure all this out will be to look at their astrological chart. The Element that your sign falls under is the physical element that will be most effective for you. Algae's may provide sufficient nutrients for water signs. for air signs, look to the fruits that grow high above the ground. Fire signs should look to foods that grow in tropical places, and lastly earth signs should look to vegetables that are harvested from below the surface. This is another responsibility that you have not yet acknowledged."

"Your sleeping habits will change a great deal depending on the responsibilities you hold in the moment. You may go for long periods of time sleeping very little. Then you may sleep for a week and not wake up. Some of these habits will be for your own protection. When earth is passing through intense planetary energies, or when you pass through an intense segment of the photon belt you may sleep more than usual. This will be so that you don't have to expend more energy than necessary, due to the amount of energy it takes you to transform. Over the next few years it is of utter importance to listen to your bodies and hearts as much as possible, to make this transition as easy as possible for you."

"Something that shall expand to its maximum, is your knowing. This is really what ascension is all about. You will no longer believe what you are being told, unless it is the truth. Eventually you shall see through the illusions and the lies that have existed on earth for centuries, and this is when you will start to feel alone. When all you have known turns out to be a lie, this is when your sense of betrayal will set in. But this is the time when you must remember that earth is only a stage and you are just an actor in the drama. This is the most powerful time for you to be able to rewrite your own script. As you realize that you pull your own strings and there is no puppeteer to manipulate you, Then and only then can you consciously create the life you want. So for those that are evolved, this is the time that they shall recognize they must own their power. For those that are younger souls, they shall feel disillusioned and cheated, or they shall fall victim to their own fears. Within either case all will be right and those who have chosen to stay will, the others will cross dimensions to the new Earth."

"Much of the physical changes you shall experience will be felt relative to the issues that you are going through at the time. Their will be a loss of connection to the physical body. You may start seeing it as your vehicle instead of your beingness. Therefore more of you will start to treat your bodies better if it is something you do not associate with your own self abuse. It you have issues of pain and fear then you may experience some of these changes painfully. You may feel as though your skull is changing shape. This is a requirement to allow for a fuller range of energies to enter the crown chakra. The heart may start to palpitate and race as though you are having a heart attack, with this there may also be an opening in this chakra that will lead to the resetting of your clock with universal time instead of earth time. Thyroid problems will become rampant as your soul urges you to speak your truth. Inevitably the heart chakra will merge with the throat chakra. This is so you will be able to speak your truth with love."

"The sexual chakra and the root chakra will also be merging. This will happen to remove you from your purely primal beliefs about sexuality, and give you the opportunity to see what spiritual creativity is. For the last twenty five thousand years you have used your sexual energies to create other life forms, not realizing that sexual energy is the creative energy of all ventures. You have used this energy as an outward expression of release rather than a conscious internal expression of creation. It is now that you will start to become consciously aware of the sexual energy within yourselves that comes from the core of the earth."

"Earth's sexual energies are close to depletion, that is why she is drying up. It is for you to stop drawing on her now and take responsibility for your own Universal supply. It is also by drawing sexual energy from sources beyond earth, that you are allowing so many star children to be born. So it is very important that you accept this change gratefully and understand sperm and ovum do not create children, it is love and the energy of orgasm that opens the door for a healthy soul, that is the real point of conception."

"Yes, this is a very new thought to you, but remember, you are going beyond human and into truth now, your self inflicted limitations must disappear for you to progress. These ideas are not new ones, these are the truths of Universal law. It is through these laws that the Lemurians and the ill fated Atlanteans were able to create your perception of super beings. They didn't know what it was like to be human, and so they didn't act as if they were. You are the only ones who can change the future of this planet. And the open time frame for this decision to be made is within the next few years of your time. You personally have made the decision to go beyond human so as you do this you can expect to do some intense processing. By nature you are stubborn, this has been a survival tactic for you. This part of your DNA. has maintained itself down through your line of genetics until it became a physical attribute and not just a personality characteristic. It is this quality that has allowed me to maintain the extreme age that I have attained. So all character traits eventually become a physical manifestation within the body. It is your stubbornness however that will make this processing more than difficult for you. You must work on your ability to accept change as it happens within your body and to stop defying that which you know must happen. Much of your ability to survive the coming times will depend on your mental and emotional flexibility and the ability to decipher actions into categories of relevance."

"The actions you deem relevant will have more direct effect over your emotions and actions, whether they be progressive or detrimental. The actions that are irrelevant can be ignored as issues belonging to others, and therefore relatively ineffectual. Again remember, all things will pass, if you let them. The less you let irrelevant action affect you, the quicker you go beyond human. Do not mourn over the loss of your humanness, but understand and desire the attributes that you gain in going beyond. You as humans do not truly understand the premise of progress yet, you are still consumed by technology. This we understand, for this is where we made our mistakes."

"Keep your full attention in the present, and take the loving advice that is offered to you from the future, take this knowledge with you into your past and rewrite your history into what it should be for your progress. It is in this way you can speed up your own future history and become that which you are supposed to be. You must release your past, it is by remembering your past that you can define the patterns that you still hold and recognized to be your personality. Release your past and you will own your future. But you can only do this from the present. The present is your open doorway to travel the corridors of time. You shall find that as you master time travel you must experience time as a vibration that exists currently. You cannot travel backwards in time and still think of your self as being from the future and expect to change the past. That is why we have sought out those who live in your time to change the future. We know we cannot change the path of events as they happened before our time. But with our knowledge of the future we can contact a form of ourselves and merge energies to have an effect on the past through our present and therefore have the ability to create and effect in this way."

"Our present is crumbling, most are dead already, that is why we have chosen to stay here caught in between time and space. If we go back to our present, we shall not live, if we stay here we shall not live. But it is better to die knowing you have completed your karma, than to run from fate. So as each one of you decide to take responsibility for your futures and make a better planet to live on, one of us disappears. You have changed the state of future existence, and the future some of you are choosing for yourselves, is not a future we are a part of. So there are relatively few of us left. Those of us who chose to come back to your space did so to try and save our race. It was the only logical move to make, but what we didn't understand was that it was also a form of compassion. It is through the interaction with you that we have come to understand that emotion is the requirement for progress on a positive level. Some of us have started to gain minimal amounts of emotion recently, due to our interaction with you. We do not know how this is affecting us but we do understand why we became unable to conceive, based on the energy configurations of emotion and our lack of them."

"Many fear emotion, but it is your key to survival. It is also the most powerful weapon there is that will be used against you. Do not fear your emotions. It is only by allowing yourself the feeling and discovering of them that you will learn what is real and then be able to differentiate between false emotion that has been planted as a weapon and real emotion that is owned as personal power. Once this is learned you shall be able to decipher between illusion and truth in all events that occur. This will be very helpful in handling irrelevant holograms that will be planted to provoke fear."

"Once you have mastered this in your own energy field, nothing can effect you if you do not let it. If you can learn to accept yourselves as energy and not just physical bodies, you shall be one step closer to the truth of who you are. This will also give you the ability to use all your energy bodies in your progress through life. You will find that many other beings live and exist within the realm of your field, but not within the physical. You are a multidimensional being. Your physical body exists within the third dimension. Your mental body exists within the fourth. The emotional body exists within the fifth and your spiritual being is the combination of all of these and more. This is why your science cannot find the source of emotion. It is not a chemical reaction, but it does produce one. Those who study the mind have been able to see the reaction to thought but not the thought itself. All these things occur because they have only learned to search within one dimension as of yet."

"What is not commonly known by the people is that there is technology that is being developed that deals with other dimensional space to create actions and reactions in them. This is why it is so important to develop a full and complete understanding of the self, it is in this way and this way only that you shall come to understand the self. And in this way you will know of the deceptions that will take place. Truth is reality, this is what you must train yourself to perceive. Many of you do not want to know the truth and this is why reality is so illusive to you. Now, we must go, your energies are becoming depleted, and we do not wish this." Just like that they were gone again.

Change, so much change. I wondered if the world could handle it. I wondered if I could handle it. In my younger years I hated change, but as I have gotten older I have come to hate stagnation. No I am not the type that moves my furniture around in my home once a week. But if life is not constantly changing I do become bored. I find that what brings the most change into my life is people. This is what I would miss the most when I left Arizona. All my life I had been judged by others. People in my home town where I grew up seemed to develop an opinion of me before they even met me, and if I didn't meet their expectations, I was somehow false or deceiving them. So I always felt as though I had to perform in one way or another. But here in Arizona no one knew me, I didn't have to be someone else's perception. The funny thing was that these people had accepted me for who I was and not what they thought I should be. There was no criticisms and no lies, just the raw truth. I found that this is really what I liked in life and I didn't want it to change.

I knew I would be leaving Arizona within a week or so, but I really didn't want to think about it. I didn't want to go home. After being in a place that was so open to discussing consciousness, I wasn't sure if I would survive back in the place that I had come from. I also knew that going home wasn't going to be easy because there were a lot of things I had left unfinished. I am the first to admit that I am a procrastinator and I had put these things off long enough. I knew that

I was going home a different person than I had left, and I wasn't sure the people I had known would be able to understand that. I was going home to the cold as well. I hate the cold, my physical composition is not well suited to it. I could think of thousands of excuses not to go home, but I knew I had to. Everyone's life had changed over the past while and I guess I was scared. I did know that going home was the only thing I could do. I also knew that I was taking a line of energy home with me that was not necessarily well established back where I had come from. So perhaps it was as much a request of the planet that I return, as it was that I take the knowledge of what I had learned and share it with others. Either way within a day or so I started packing and praying that my car would get me home.

My car was actually happy to be going home. It didn't like the heat in Arizona in the summertime, so that was a plus. I figured if my car was happy, I was twice as likely to get home with no problems. So over the course of the next few days I made the effort to get around to see those I hadn't seen in awhile to say good-bye. I hate good-byes, they sound so final. I much prefer, see you later. After all we will see everyone again at some time. The last few days I was in the desert, I tried to absorb as much of it as I possibly could, so I could take it with me. I chose a route that would take me home in a different manner than I had driven there, and with that done I was already to leave.

My experience of Arizona would not be one that I would ever forget, but little did I know then that it would also be an ongoing one. As I drove beyond the Tucson city limits I started to cry with gratefulness, sadness and joy. There were so many emotions running through me that I couldn't feel one at a time. I eventually had to pull the car over so I could finish crying. I felt as though I was leaving my heart behind. I didn't think it would be this difficult to leave. Within a few minutes I managed to regain my composure and got back on the highway. By this time it was dark and I could see Tucson lit up in all its glory in the rear view mirror. But there was something else I could see. It was a ship, and it looked like it was following me. I kept checking my mirror but even after a half hour the ship was still there, then a minute later it disappeared. I thought that was very touching of them to give me an escort out of the city. The desert at night can be very black except for the stars that light up the night sky. As I drove and watched the stars disappear beyond the range of my window I thought of how blessed I had been to go through what I had gone through in this magical place of Arizona. I did wonder if I would ever be able to settle down again. I felt as though somehow this trip had confirmed the gypsy in my soul. Then as I rounded the next corner I came to a dead stop. There in front of my car was the ship that had been following me earlier. As I got out of the car and approached the ship I saw that three beings stood in front of it. The one I recognized as the Grey with the jewel in his forehead. The other was a being I worked with that I had come to know as Tall One. But the other one I did not recognize. I was a beautiful gold shimmering energy, with ribbons of white light that flowed and danced within the gold. And around this energy was a hue of breathtaking turquoise that seemed to soothe the soul. As I stood in front of the Alien being he began to speak.

"We have come to let you know that you do not go alone. We are with you on every step of your journey. You have restructured your energy while you have been here with us, and this allows us to return to your home with you. We would have been with you always, but this allows for interaction on a more personal level. It also allows for interaction with others that will be open to your story. We are only a thought away and this is what we wish you to know. Do not fear going back to the place of your birth, we are a part of your family now. You feel you are unfamiliar with the gold energy here. This we have brought to you as a gift. It is time now for you to see your own soul. That is what this energy is. You feel it is far too beautiful for you but this is who you are. And now you must integrate it. Open yourself and allow the higher you into the body."

As I did this I could feel nothing but complete and total love. I could feel myself merge with the beings that stood in front of me, and I could feel a merging with all the people I loved on this planet. I knew then that I am a part of these people always and forever. I could leave my fear and know that I am safe. The job I had to do on this planet was far too important for me to get caught up in self pity or anger, because I couldn't stay in Tucson. I had never felt my own soul as I did now, and I knew this was a feeling I wanted to keep. This I thought was the feeling of heaven. It took a while for me to come back to earth, and I didn't know how much time had elapsed. I thought that the ship must be holding up a great deal of traffic, but to my amazement there was not a car in sight. So I got back in my car and proceeded to drive, along my route back to Canada. But within minutes my car started to over heat so I had to pull over and let it rest.

As I sat there talking to my car about why it had overheated, the only response I got was that it wasn't used to the new vibration of my body and I had been responsible for it overloading. I apologized and did some work with its internal workings. After a couple of hours it was ready to go again, and so I was back on the road. I am the kind of traveller that prefers to travel at night. The highways are less crowded and it is cooler, especially in the summer. On the trip home I didn't seem to require resting, I am not sure if this was because of the new integration that had just happened or if it was just that I had wanted to get this over with. Either way, before I knew it I was back at the Canadian border and in my home province of Ontario.

It is always an amazement to me how the seasons change so fast as you travel north. This had been the first time I had ever experienced the sunny south, and it was very easy to see why it was so alluring for people. When I had originally left Canada, within the first twenty four hours, I had gone from winter conditions to late summer. This is very hard on your body. I adjusted extremely well, and very quickly. But going home would be a different matter.

One of the major differences between Canada and the US, is the amount of people that populated this country. The first few days that I had been in the U.S. I was almost claustrophobic. There were people everywhere and as you move down the highway, every ten minutes there is a truck stop, or a food rest stop of some kind. The closer I got to home, the longer distance I would travel with nothing except road signs to keep me company. I realized then what a vast expanse this country was. The place of my birth was only moments away and I still didn't really want to be here.

I had envisioned what it would feel like to drive up the old familiar roads that I had travelled for years, and I had thought it would feel better than it did. I had found something in Arizona that had been missing all my life. I had found self acceptance there, and I wasn't sure if I would be able to find it here. But I was thankful of one thing, at least now I new what acceptance felt like, and I knew I wouldn't stop until I had that feeling again. There was a lot of people in this area that were like me, maybe it is time for us to join together and make a statement that we have the right to our own beliefs, and that there should be no reason to fear what we believe.

I knew in my mind I was just trying to make this whole thing feel better. In my life I had run up against obstacles in the form of people's opinions, I was amazed at how much I still let it provoke me. I had learned so much in the past short while.

As I approached my home town, population of fifteen thousand, my attention was drawn upward. There in the sky above the town and extending to the north, was a giant golden pyramid. I slowed down and pulled the car over to the side of the road. I couldn't believe what I was seeing. I rubbed my eyes, and then I blinked not trusting what I saw. But the pyramid just hung there beaming with golden light, for miles and miles. I took that as a sign that I was in the right place whether I liked it or not, and somehow I knew that my life would be focused in this area, at least for awhile. As I tried to make some peace with being home again, a voice came into my head, and this is what it said,"You are a part of this. The energies of the grid system are changing. By coming home you have allowed some of these energies to complete this movement. This is your birth place but it is not your home. You are not of this planet. you are an energy being that exists within a consciousness, you have volunteered to be here. And this is where you must start to do the work you came here to do. Here in this place, this is birthing energy, new events can be created. You have a new life now. You have chosen your direction and it is here that it is to be started. Allow yourself to love all those who would give you grief. Take the knowledge you now have and seek out those who wish to share it. It is within this process that you will discover your family, even here in this place. Do not fear. Love and you will have love returned to you."

I think I needed that little reminder. All of a sudden I realized that I was no where near my home, I guess I had just been tapping into the dream state for awhile. I had been on the road for quite a few hours, and I knew my fears were running me at this time. And perhaps I was feeling a little abandoned by the beings I had been so intimate with for the last long while. It was the boost that I needed to continue on this trip. I also realized all of the memories I had from childhood were trying to creep in to my mind right now as well. It has always amazed me how my conditioning sticks with me. The fears that people helped instill in you, when you were a child, can crop up at the most unexpected times.

I was so thankful for the words of guidance, I found myself driving down the road and thanking the grass and the trees, anything I could think of to thank. All this stuff that I kept being told about my destiny, seemed like an illusion to me. I almost couldn't conceive of being what they said I was. yet I knew I had a specific goal to achieve in life, even if I still wasn't sure what it was. I had always thought that I was a meant to be child. I was born into a family of six children, but I was born eight years behind my brother. I was very much a surprise, and from what I can understand my birth created some turbulence in the family.

Growing up was difficult, I lived in a world that I thought was magical, but because of the severe dysfunction of my family, my life became hard and cold. I believe everyone on this earth is an abuse survivor of some kind and the abuse within my family was pretty severe. It took me years to make any kind of peace with what had happened to me. It was only when I came to understand the concept of karma that I accepted the responsibility of what had happened to me as a child and started to change the negative programming.

Enduring that abuse had taught me to take my mind out of my body and go elsewhere. I believe it is one of the reasons I was fortunate enough, to be able to have these interactions with these other beings. Even though I was aware of having made some peace with my past, I knew being home would still provoke me. I knew, that this whole experience in Arizona, was just the beginning. It was time to stop running. All my life I had run to avoid myself. I knew I couldn't do that anymore. So now that I was home, I knew I would learn many lessons about who my friends really were. I also knew I would find out who my family were. So with this in mind, and not wanting to deal with rush hour traffic in Toronto, I decided to stop and see some friends in the city. In the morning I would find myself braver and so I left for the place I had grown up, the place I would be calling home.

Chapter Eight

Home! I was home. I could say that as many times as I wanted, I just couldn't feel it. The truth of the matter was, I had been more at home in Arizona than I had ever been in Huntsville. It was a new experience for me to have been unconditionally accepted by people and treated as their family. Being back in Huntsville, somehow felt like being back in the land of judgement. Huntsville was a home built from fear for me. The more I could feel the old fears creep back into my psyche, the more I understood why I was actually back here. This really was the perfect place for me to return to, if I was to process my beliefs around fear.

I was beginning to realize that perhaps I had only been given breathing room in Arizona. A lot of the issues I thought I had eliminated, I hadn't, but I had been able to see what it was like to live without them, and that was a feeling I wanted to return to. I had a taste of paradise and knew that paradise could be achieved. The trick in this situation was to recreate it for myself, in what I felt to be a harsh environment.

Because of my religious upbringing, many times when I am in a situation like this, a specific quote from the bible enters my mind to give me a jolt. This circumstance was no different from any other. The quote that came to mind this time was,"Judge lest ye be judged." Maybe that was right. I had been away for awhile. People are constantly changing. I had changed and maybe people would react to that change instead of just reacting to their pre programmed memory of me. Either way I had to go with that thought. I have always found the bible to be an amazing document because of the truths it contains. My only problem with it, is not the book itself, but the extremely limited translation that mankind has literally misinterpreted it to be.

I had found a job out of town, and so I didn't see too many people. That was what I needed. A slow integration process was the best right now. I had so much information I wasn't sure how they would react to me informing them of the truth of my journey. I knew some people would just go into overload and shut down. Others would feed on what I knew, and they would pursue me. Then others would accept it as part of their own knowing, whether they had been aware of it or not previously. I was finding myself getting overly exhausted very quickly here. The energy was so heavy compared to Arizona. Being here was like carrying an extra fifty pounds on your back.

The humidity had taken its toll as well. I was having much greater problems integrating my so called home than I ever did my second home. Since I was a child I had always made the statement that I had been born in the wrong place. The problems that I was going through were proving that to me now. It took me a good three weeks to start getting comfortable again. All the old physical problems started to return as well. The ache I get in my body with the onset of the least bit of cold. The stuffiness in the sinuses because of the humidity. So many things I forgot about while I was away had suddenly returned. The people in Arizona have no idea how good life is there, but I knew I was here for a reason, I was just hoping that I wasn't going to be here for very long. I missed my friends and the climate that I felt were waiting for me, three thousand miles away. I didn't really want to see another Canadian winter either. I wanted to go home. That thought just kept bringing me to tears.

The one thing that was positive this time was, that I seemed to be attracting a whole new crowd of people. People that were at least interested in what I had to say. Not all of them agreed with the words that I used, but most understood the principle of what was intended. I found myself doing quite a bit of travelling to talk to groups, and do private sessions with people about Aliens and the future. I was even doing conference calls with people from all over the world. All this was very strange for me. In this place that I had been born to, I had gone from being a target for angry retribution, to being someone that was respected within a certain circle.

I was happy about this. This felt very good for me. Finally, a feeling of some kind of acceptance in the place that was supposed to be my home. Maybe I was starting to develop some kind of family here. After all, family is by love and not by blood. Maybe I could learn to live here again. But as soon as I had that thought, I knew that if I had the opportunity to return to Arizona, I would take it in a flash.

I was only fooling myself. I still really didn't want to be here, my heart was in Arizona.

Within two months of being home, complete depression had set in. I had no energy, I was in constant pain from an unknown source. I really just wanted to die. I hated my life, it just wasn't worth living. I was lonely and I was scared. Hate anger and fear ruled me. I was miserable and I didn't know how to get out of it. All I could do is cry. I felt totally abandoned by my Alien friends and life in general. Death was looking to be a very attractive alternative. How could I have gone from being on such a high to feeling as though I was in the depths of hell?

Time didn't seem to be moving. This feeling just kept lingering and clinging to me. I was alone. No one here understood me. I had no one to talk to. Everyone just wanted me for what they could get out of me. I knew there were exceptions to this but that is the way I felt in general. I felt like people were just using me to stir up some excitement in their boring lives. No one really took me seriously about the changes that had to be made in their lives to bring about the changes that have to be made in this world. Even though none of this was a reality from the point of the other person, it was the reality I was choosing to live in. I was living in self pity.

And then I remembered what the Alien had said "You will die in self pity." I knew I didn't really want to die. I was just having a desperately hard time dealing with the changes that had happened within me. I was someone else now. I hadn't really understood how different I had become until I did come home. Now I felt like I was the Alien in a foreign world. It was when I had that thought, that everything started to change for me. It was then that all of this started to make some sense to me.

These Aliens are simply an aspect of ourselves, but they represent an aspect that we don't really want to look at. It is a peak into the absolute in desensitization. It is a very revealing look at what we are becoming and most people don't want to look at it when they can still change it. They only agree to see it when it is to late. That way they can blame someone or something else. In this way they avoid responsibility for their own lives. In essence they fall victim to their own Alien. The Alien within. We have all determined part of ourselves to be Alien. Whether it is the psychic ability that is inherent in all of us, or whether it is something as simple as love. If we don't want to deal with it then it becomes our Alien.

So not only did we take the reflection of ourselves as desensitized humans to the extreme lo create the Greys. we have manifested our fear of love in the destruction of this planet We now treat our own planet as if it were an Alien being. Once we were in tune with the planet, we treated her with honour and respect. Now we have allowed society to deem who or what deserves respect. We have categorized normal and abnormal. That is the attitude that runs the world now. If it is not the media's version of normal, then it is wrong, not simply different. So many people need to be told what to think before they give themselves permission to think.

We have eliminated the power of uniqueness within those limiting lines of normal. Our lines of normal have kept us safe and made sure that no one can make waves or change anything. We have become so conditioned that we now treat our own instincts and intuition as Alien. Even the word is severe. Official documentation refers to people from other lands as Aliens, even though they still live on this planet. Now is that a statement in subtlety or what? If it is not the narrow pointed view of normal, then it is Alien, and if it is Alien, it is wrong. And most things that are wrong, are judged to be eliminated.

We have forgotten that we are multi-dimensional beings, and that we have eliminated our Aliens to the point that we only acknowledge this shell that we live in. We are even told to control our emotions. Only in this sense it means, don't let them show if they are anything other than happy. Instead they should be subdued to the point of extinction. Remember extinction is forever, and when emotions are gone forever, we become the Greys. Those that we are so afraid of now. Those that are trying to help us make peace with our own Aliens. Nothing is truly Alien to us if we don't see it as being wrong or foreign from ourselves.

The inability to allow all parts of ourselves to be integrated into one beingness, is giving all of us split personalities and other forms of psychosis. We are saying that some parts of us are right and some are wrong, when it takes all parts to make who we are. We are far too quick to judge someone else, or see their faults without first looking at ourselves. We have the attitude that if we can make other people change to what we think they should be, then we don't have to change ourselves.

As I was starting to understand all of this, I also understood it was my own denial or nonacceptance of my own Aliens that was making me miserable. I was not allowing me to feel myself, or my own emotions, therefore I was projecting my anger onto others so I didn't have to do the work required to change my own attitude. It wasn't laziness, it was fear. It was fear of of fully stepping into the whole of my being. What if I couldn't merge all the parts of myself successfully? Or what if I couldn't be the person I was supposed to be and the universe became disappointed in me? I wasn't sure if I could live with that, but I knew for sure that I couldn't live with myself if I didn't try.

Enough of this feeling sorry for myself. I had made a conscious decision to dedicate my life to waking up love on this planet. I knew what I was getting into when I did it, I knew I had a responsibility to fulfil and all I could do is try. After all success is not really in achieving your goal, it is in the journey to the goal. You can achieve anything but first you must apply yourself in that direction. How would I be able to go out into the world and tell people what needs to be done to bring about change, if I wasn't in the process of doing what I had to do as well? People do not learn by telling them what to do, they only learn whats possible when they see it has already been done.

The old saying is, "Seeing is believing," my personal version has become "Trust in what you believe, to see." When it comes to other dimensional interactions, it will take believing to help you see. This is only one of the reasons children see so much. As a child you have not yet leaned to disbelieve your eyes. It is only through much conditioned response from others that "That's not real" becomes part of your belief system. It is when you start to understand what that really means, that you stop seeing what you had seen all along. This becomes one of our major lessons in not trusting ourselves. We need to start really trusting ourselves and what is real and true for us and this planet so that we cannot be mislead by the opinions of others, that may not have our highest good as their greatest consideration.

Only by having trust in ourselves as an adult are we going to be able to allow our children to maintain the trust in themselves that they will need to take them into the future. As adults we have the responsibility to show the children that we want them to experience freedom as we have never experienced it before. If we allow them freedom in their vision perhaps they will teach us to see in a way we haven't yet allowed ourselves too, and in this way we will create a new future. Do we really want to teach the children to give their power away, or do we want them to be able to own their power and use it to create a world we would be proud to live upon?

All the components are still here in us, they just have to be activated. All these different musings were leading me to a space of thoughtfulness, with just a tinge of happiness thrown in. The depression was lifting and I wasn't sure where I was going but I knew I had to go. So I started to let go and just let life happen.

Entertaining yourself in the winter can be a huge job when winter lasts for six months of the year. My Alien friends had returned to some degree and were helping me to integrate many of the learning's I had absorbed in Arizona. To do this, I was starting to live in a meditative state. I would spent a lot of time laying down in that space between waking and sleeping. Aware of what was around me, but consciously another place.

I was off in other parts of the world, or other parts of the universe. I was very busy being educated in Universal laws and how they functioned here on Earth. If I wasn't doing this, I was helping people or other beings that were in a state of stress due to plane crashes or earthquakes or other disasters. Some of the things I was doing were hard for me to believe, but there they were right in front of my eyes. Sometimes I just bore witness to the lives of others and how their beliefs structured their reality.

It was early spring when my emotions started to get a little crazy again. Up and down and all over the place, it was then that my friend with the crystal in his forehead decided to grace my life with his presence.

"I can see you are out of control once again. You sit and think so much about why this is happening to you. You are not even sure what is happening to you. This water falls from your eyes in the form of tears, and then you rage, hating all things in your line of sight. You are completely exhausted from trying to battle yourself."

"Your questions are not in vain, this is something you must go through so that you shall recognize the energy when you see it in others. This, what you are feeling, is the energy of being indecisive. You have not made your contract to stay here on earth and assist people through the changes to come, or die and leave the job for someone else. You had assumed that since you dedicated your life to love, that it automatically meant you were to stay on earth. This is not so. You must consciously desire to stay here, if you wish to live. Even if you choose death, you will still be able to help through the changes, it will however be in a different vibration. You have free will to choose whatever you want. There is no judgement passed, no matter what decision you arrive upon. For you to return to emotional stability, you must make a conscious decision. You will have three days to do this. During this time you will be allowed to see into much of your future, this is so that your decision will be an informed one. Once this decision is made it will affect many more people than just yourself. However you must make this decision based on your own desires. You must know that you have been destined for a specific future since long before you were born. You took a very long time to design this lifetime to be of the greatest advantage for the people. You are not in this lifetime for yourself as much as you are here for the people. This will take you some time to accept. You have always been very reclusive, and in many ways elusive, to yourself and others. All this will change if you decide to stay. You see that I have faded to merely a shadow of the being you first met. The decision you make will affect me directly. I will leave you now. Go to your sacred space and allow yourself to see the future that awaits you. Make your decision, and when that is done I shall return. There is more information that you need to remember, but the time is not now. Go. Sign your contracts with fate. I am here to support you in your decision."

Live or die? Of course I want to live, don't I? I was starting to realize more and more, how subconscious so much of this stuff was. I would have to delve deep into my soul for the answer to this one. I was more than aware that many times in my life I was wishing that I could get off of this planet But to actually think about terminating my existence here, that was another matter. Most of the time when we think about death, it is because we really can't imagine it happening. So there is some kind of safety in thinking about it. To give serious thought about not seeing the sun rise anymore, or hearing the sounds of thunder, that was not what I wanted. However on the other hand, did I really want to go through what I was scheduled to do in a physical vibration. It would be so easy for me to just disappear and help people from a safe space. It was then that I realized what I was really doing. I was afraid for myself and my own well being. If I stayed I would be able to set some kind of example for those that would be going through the same thing as I was. The desire to leave actually came from a fear of being responsible for my actions. Once again I saw the pattern of being afraid to claim my power from a soul level, and use it through the physical body. This fear as I was realizing came from a place so deep within myself that it would take time and processing to be able to release it completely.

So within twenty four hours I had made my decision, and that was to stay. I literally sat down and made out a contract to do whatever it was that I was supposed to do here on planet earth for the time I had to be here. I dated it and signed it as though it was any other contact. Minutes later it felt as though a few thousand pounds was lifted from my shoulders as I was able to breath deeply again. As I started to feel the pleasure that truly exists in simply breathing I could feel the heavy weighted presence of tiredness looming down upon me. This tiredness was not the tiredness you would feel after a long hard days work. but more what you would feel after a week of not sleeping. It was in the middle of the day but I knew I must sleep, I knew I was being called elsewhere for reasons yet to be revealed. So I lay down on the bed. and I do not recall closing my eyes. Instantly I was back aboard the ship and in front of me stood my Alien friend. He was becoming continuously more transparent to my physical eyes. But in my mind his voice seemed to be stronger than ever.

"Good we are very pleased that you have made this decision. As you can see, my time to take up physical space in this body has almost ended. This as well, is good. Our existence has served its purpose for you especially. It is now that I can say my life is a success. By the decision you have made to stay and do the job you were born to do, you have consciously erased my existence. Do not feel bad or guilty about this. This is a victory for us. You have changed the future so that you do not end up as one of us. You still have many other potential futures but they are of your choosing. You have conquered the greatest challenge within yourself. That was the challenge of fear. You have chosen to feel emotion. You have chosen to control your own existence. You have fulfilled your karmic burdens. You may now go through a time period of feeling completely empty, or completely lost. You live your whole life based on what you believe. Beliefs are like the rule book that create the blueprint for your existence. In certain ways you could link beliefs to karma, and karma to DNA. Each person is different, but they are the same as well. So your entire life is designed around the lessons you must learn on a karmic level. Once you have eliminated that karma, there is a void or the feeling of emptiness, left in your existence. Many people interpret this as death, and some are so literal that they do chose to exit the planet. However in most, it is like the lack of purpose in life, or the feeling of not having a direction anymore. One of the other things that you must be very aware of at this point, is that for you now, karma will be almost instant. Since earth is coming to its consciousness shifting point, there is no time to waste, you shall see the ramifications of your actions very quickly and with intensity. How you create your life is quite literally in your hands, but without the obligation to learn certain lessons on a karmic level. It is at this point where you are no longer bound by the same rules you have been bound to in the past. Your rules are no longer the rules made by men. You now are only confined to Universal laws and your own insecurities. This is where you will process all your own personal issues, so that you may rewrite your rules of existence. It is now that you have full power to decide how difficult or easy your life will be. Your life is now based in personal issues and what it is you feel you must accomplish to find joy. The structure of your life is now built on what you think you believe, both positive and negative. If you believe you life is a struggle, then it will be."

"The opposite belief applies as well. But you must go to a core level to know what it is that you believe. For it is now that the ego will feel most threatened by the soul. Your ego will fear loss of its existence, and replacement by the soul. It will do its best to not allow you to come to a place of peace. Deal with it as you would a child. Reason with it, let it know that it will always be a part of you, ease its fears. It is an entity within itself and it is real. Talk to it as you would a friend. Remember it has kept you alive at times when you needed it, it has played an important role in your life. It should be honored for the service it has offered you. It offered you security when you needed it, now it is time to offer it security, as it fears its own death. When the ego can be appeased, and allowed to see that there is no such thing as death, then you shall truly understand the principle of oneness. You need your ego to help you create the illusion of separation. But do not be surprised when you find out what oneness really is. The reason that the ego created the illusion of separation is that, it fears loss of self or self identity. I am quite sure that you will be very surprised at the truth of oneness, once you have achieved it. Remember that you are now entering the most powerful time of your physical existence here on earth. You will find out what you truly believe at a cellular level. All the veils will fall away now and you shall have true vision. The world that you have known will cease to exist in many ways. Much of what you will go through may be difficult, because of the feeling that none of what you see on the planet makes sense. You will start interpreting the actions of the people as one huge karmic dance. It will become crystal clear for you. As it does, your desire to leave the planet may become great. When this happens remember that you are starting to remember where it is that you came from. The more you remember where you came from. the more empowered you become. It is then that you will be able to use your knowing of energy to start recreating your world on a different level. But to get to this point you may first have to clear any and all negative belief structures that exist in your being. Once this is done you may not be able to see the physical actions of earth anymore. What you will be able to see is the energetic action behind the physical reaction."

"The world that you will live in will be very different than the mass amount of peoples that exist presently. You shall see everything from a different dimensional level. For you, all explanations for physical causes will be based in the emotional or spiritual realms, and this is the realm of unseen energy. You will discover the law of energetics. This will lead you to understanding all the so called miracles that the one called Christ could perform. You have chosen to go beyond human, and so you shall also experience your physical existence in this way. You write your own rules now, and there is nothing you can't do if first you believe. Do not be disturbed by the comments of others that are dismayed because you do not understand life as they do. Do not think you are missing something. Know that this is what you have chosen and it is only in this way that earth will be on its way to making a positive shift. The others that may try to make you feel like an outsider only feel threatened by your presence, because it triggers the memory of obligation in them. These people fear change and they would conform and control you if they could. But because you are beyond your karma, and on a subconscious level they know this, they know that you are free, and they have anger at themselves for not completing there own karma yet. So it is actually a form of spiritual envy that will make them dislike you or make you fee unwelcome. Pay no attention to this. Offer them love and wish them well on their journey. For in this time it is too important that you do the job you came here to do. You are here as a teacher and a keeper. It is for you to assist the others that will go through this process at different times over the coming years. You are here to help inform the others of events that do occur on different dimensional levels. Part of your job is to help others think in a manner that will expand their conscious dimensional existence. But the most important thing that you are here doing is just simply being by allowing your memory of who you are to come to the surface and be reflected in your actions. You carry transitional energy, that means that all you cross and all you touch shall be changed in some way by your presence. However only those that desire change shall call you into their lives. Go gracefully, knowing that they have yet to deal with what you have already gone through. Compassion, patience and love is all you shall need to have a peaceful existence, and to do the job you came to do. Do not get angry at those who cannot understand your form of existence, perhaps they never will, so do not punish them or your self. Acceptance is the only way you shall be able to offer people assistance in changing their lives. You must first accept what is, to be able to create a future vision. The only place you truly ever work from is the present. Once you understand the power that is in the present, then you will be able to create your future, and in doing so,

135

influence your past. You have the ability to release the past that was and adjust a new one to fit your future. But to do this, you must truly forgive yourself and all others, that you would claim to fall victim to. By releasing yourself from fear, you set yourself free from the confines of time. It is then that future or past no longer exist. There is only now. The time has come for me to leave. I will always be with you on an energetic level. You just shall not visit with me here on the ship anymore. It would honour me greatly if you allowed me to exit through you. The merging of my past and your future would come to a resting place in the now. By your will I shall pass through you, and complete my destiny."

I stood there in a state of shock not wanting my friend to go, but wanting to release him all at the same time. So after a silent moment I motioned to him to come forward and pass through me. The tears started to role down my cheeks as I knew I would never see him in this way again. All things will die, but nothing ever ends.

As he drew close I could feel his energy change and as he moved through the front of my body. I saw him in his true form. He was beautiful golden light that seemed to beam all directions with ongoing waves. I looked at the light and knew it to be my own being that was merging with me through my heart. All along he had been an aspect of me. But it wasn't til the end, that I stopped seeing a separate entity, and started to accept him as part of who I am. My refusal to accept all parts of me had created the physical manifestation of the Alien. By refusing to allow our emotions we can create a future based on the lack of it. Or we can integrate our feelings and honour them for the great service they provide. By doing this we eliminate our Aliens within. We stop separating ourselves from our souls. And with this thought the integration of my Alien self with my inner self, was complete. I had literally accepted my own Alien nature, and so he could not exist anymore. We are now parts of one another created by acceptance. We are both more complete beings for having allowed love to over shadow each others differences.

In the beginning I was terrified of the Aliens and of my own emotion. I was afraid of losing control. I was shown in a very literal way what happens when we fear our own inner selves. We have a deep core belief that anything external to ourselves is out of our control, and so we have allowed our physical reality to use time and space to create the illusion of separation. That is why these beings were the Greys. They were neither black or white. They were neutral. Now I was able to feel my friend the Alien within me, instead of my enemy the Alien. I had found a form of peace, and I knew he had too.

The only sadness came from looking forward to being on the ship, if for no other reason than it got me off this planet. Not that I hate this planet but sometimes it is very wearing on the nerves, and for me, having been on the ship was like taking a little holiday. I also realized that having the type of revelations I did while I was with him would change as well. Over the past two years, so much of the excitement had come out of discovering the new path I was on. There was really nothing different. It is like starting a new job. In the beginning everything is new and wondrous. The challenge of learning is everywhere, but as time passes and you have learned the new things and integrated them, it just becomes part of your beingness. This is what was happening to me. What had been so magical for me in the beginning was now becoming normal.

In a way, I was very proud of this, because it meant that I believed in a new way of thinking. I was living my souls purpose. But I must admit to missing the magic and excitement I felt at the beginning when all was so new, but this is the nature of life. For awhile I was wondering if I had lost my connection or not. I wasn't having anything wild or bizarre happening. Just the same old synchronicity's of having my thoughts manifest themselves physically. But then one day I realized that these were exactly the same things, that had been happening all along, it was just that I was so used to them now the I didn't perceive them as separate from me anymore. And that is the secret of oneness. It happens when you allow yourself to feel what you think, or what you know.

When you allow yourself to feel it, you stop thinking about it, and it is then that you become it, and becoming it is the goal of your soul. So many people don't think they can do anything to change this big world. That is where they are wrong. It is only by each individual making a conscious decision to create a better life for themselves and then manifesting that thought, that this earth will change. Change starts in the heart of the individual. It takes all the individuals on earth to make up the mass consciousness.

Everything starts with feeling. We first must feel it, to believe it. If we can believe it, we will automatically create it. But it all starts with feeling. I for one do not want to manifest a future as the Greys. That is what we are doing by desensitizing ourselves to the feeling experience. If we lose our ability to feel, we will become just like robots. Robots are very easy to control. If we lose our ability to feel, we will lose our ability to pro-create. There will be no more laughter from the children.

It is for us to now start exercising our right of choice. In the last while I have seen so many people going through extreme hard times. Aside from the karma that may exist these people have not made the choice to own their lives yet. I understand this as I am still in the process of learning and accepting the power of such a decision. I really wish that I could tell everyone that it is going to get better, but the fact is that it can only get better if you let it. Even when there is chaos going on all around us, we still own the energy within us, and that is the power we need to change what we don't want.

With the assistance of the Greys, and my own will, I have seen the calm that can be created within my own life when I just stand still. All things work in a cyclic nature, sometimes we chase life to the point where we will never catch it. But if we were to instead, stand still and wait, then all those we were chasing, sooner or later would come around to meet us where we were standing. It is our diehard stubbornness or the ego part of ourselves that will not let us stop. We have it stuck in our heads that to pursue is to win. When we learn the truth about who we are, then we understand what we desire comes to us. We need to be the magnet that attracts the metal.

What we must do now is allow the illusion of separateness to fall away, so that we may help this planet and ourselves transform in a painless rebirth. The planet is in full blown contractions now, about to give birth. If you have ever given birth, or have ever seen it happen, you know the pain that is involved. Right now we must hold a vision of the future.

The earth, she knows want she wants and she wishes for us all to join her in the desire for an easy birth and celebrate the coming of a happy healthy new world. We must hold the image of happiness and health, love and joy if we are to see who it is that we truly are as a race. However we can only do this by going inside and creating that space of love at the still point within us. We must feel this love to be able to project it. Many beings on this planet are in objection to unity. For unity obliterates the need for control and judgement, and therefore, fear will disappear. Far too many beings here use fear to control others, and it is those beings that will do everything in their power to circumvent peace. This is why the cry goes out all people on an individual level to access their place of power, become secure in it and then allow self healing and self love to happen.

We have become so accustomed to pain, we feel love and peace are out of reach. It is accepted that what we want is not worth it, unless we had to work for it. I say it is time for this belief system to end. We as beings on this planet have done our time struggling and suffering, we now deserve to have a time of peace and love. It is our right and our obligation to take control of our lives for the betterment of the universe. This is the place and the power of our position and responsibility towards the universe and all beings in it.

There have been so many movies over the past several years of the battle between good and evil in outer space. In more ways than we understand, it has come down to that. But the battle we really face is the one between good and evil in inner space. So many of my clients report, having the feeling of what they describe as being almost a " split personality ". This is the actualization of the tear in the fabric of time and space, this is the weaving of dimensional realities that keeps all things in balance on this planet. As this weaving becomes more separated, the two sides of our being become more distinct. With this occurring, we can be happy go lucky one moment and then moody and raging the next. We have lost the natural balance we had when this fabric was intact. It is now for us to find our balance point, so that the fabric can be joined together again.

It is always to be remembered that this earth is simply a reflection of the mental, emotional and spiritual states of the human beings that exist on it. It is just a big ball of clay that we mold with our thoughts and feelings. If you have ever travelled and gone through the experience of feeling that one place is more peaceful than another, without any explanation, then you can understand the principle I am speaking of. The land is a giant energy sponge that will absorb and hold the emotions of the people. The same principle is active when you walk into a beautiful home, but are extremely uncomfortable. It is one of two things, either you have not given yourself permission to enjoy beauty, or someone that lives there is not vibrating in a beautiful way.

What you feel, was not developed just as an inconvenience, or as warning system to pain. Your senses were developed as a form of antennae. They were originally meant for us to be able to tap into the seen and the unseen worlds that exist around us. This is what we need to awaken in ourselves once again. In the years to come there will be times when knowing the truth of a situation cannot be determined visually. Our very lives may depend on our ability to feel the situation out. This is where trust is needed. and to trust yourself is to love yourself. Knowing who you are will allow for you to go beyond fear. It is then that we will create the lives that we desire. First we must learn to use the tools that we have, and the tools we have are only as good as the person using them. Many masterpieces have been created with the bare essential tools. Love and passion made them great, not the cost of the paintbrush.

For me, passion is the one element that I exist in. I have a passion for my work. I have a passion for my life. I have a passion for my love, and I have the greatest passion for this planet and all beings on her. Passion is feeling with intensity. The more energy you learn to generate in any one direction, the more influence you shall have. I try to channel as much passion into love, as I do into my work, because for me they are one in the same. There is no separation for me. My work is my life and my life is my work and there lies my pleasure.

The vibrational frequency is rising. We are searching for answers beyond what is logical. We have developed a craving to go beyond ourselves and know truth. In the past we have tried to take our energies out of ourselves and throw them towards the Universe. We have gotten this backwards. What needs to be done to complete our cycle, is to grab hold of Universal energies and bring them down into ourselves and into our heart. It is in doing this that we will bring what is out there back into ourselves so that we shall know all is one. We have long perceived that the soul lives outside of the body. It is only then by reaching out and grabbing it. that we will draw it inside ourselves and be able to go beyond human.

If we are to create a new world that will exist beyond the year 2025, we must purge ourselves of fear and allow love to permeate every part of our being. As we do this light will flood the planet and peace will reign. The light that is trying to get in is represented by the disappearance of the ozone. The ozone has been here to protect us, until we were ready for a higher vibrational frequency. Now we are ready and it is dissipating. The powers that be scare you into protecting yourself. Of course they ask this of you. They do not want to lose control because you lose your fear. This is why there has been such an awareness campaign towards sunscreens. Skin cancer did not even start to rise until there was a fear created that the light was harmful.

All things tied to the light must be carefully monitored even the radiation off of the lights at your work place. A subconscious fear is being placed here to avoid the light. Those that are in power know that love is found in the light and that is why they are creating a huge belief system around light. If people live in the light they will lose their fear and those in control will lose their power. But if they are successful in making people afraid of the light, then those people will not seek to find their own brilliance.

The choice is ours. The years 2012, 2015, and 2025 will be three of the most powerful influential years over the next many years. My friends the Aliens have informed me of some of the events that will occur and what to watch for as media coverage leading into these events. The potential future has been mapped by those that want control. It is my desire to be free and to help others sculpt their lives based in love, so that they also may be free and experience the joy that they deserve.

My vision of the future is a beautiful one. It is one where we can interact freely with other people and other planetary beings acting as one. It is where we will come to understand and accept our soul as one with our physical being. It is where we can create a planet that is our perception of perfect. It is where we are free to love and be loved. It is a world where happiness and joy are the rule and not the exception.

This and so much more the Greys helped me to learn. I miss the physical interaction with them, but they are always with me now. I can communicate with them at any time, and they are open to communicating with others for assistance as well. It was for them, as well as for myself that I have written this book. Their help in my life has been invaluable and I wish to honour them for that. I ask nothing more now than, for you to go in love and go in peace. Know that in your heart lies the truth. Trust yourself and love yourself . We have the power to change existence as we know it, to give ourselves and our children the gift of a beautiful life. All we have to do is love ourselves and allow the joy that comes from that to be the expression of our lives.

The Update

The story you just read was written in 1996. It covered the highlights of the events that happened in the early 90's in my life. I released the book to a very limited audience at that time. So now you may be wondering why I would want to re-release a virtually unknown book as an updated version? Well it is only now that the whole story can be told. I am one of those people that always wonders what happened after all the fantastic stuff. You know, the "Where are they now?" version. Well this is exactly why I am releasing this again. Now I can tell you what happened after those incredible experiences. The story you are about to read is the human journey that happens after incredible things happen to the human.

If you are anything like me at all, you would naturally think, after those amazing experiences that a person would thrive. That their knowledge would be desired and that they would carve out their place in life with relative ease. However, that is the Hollywood version. Integrating back into everyday life is very difficult after that. It is not so much that people don't accept you, it is more that you have no idea how to accept yourself. Having experiences like those leave, big gaping holes in your ability to settle into a reality that no longer exists for you.

The things that I learned in talking with the Alien no longer allowed me to see the world as a place where I could just do a 9-5 job anymore. Some of the residual affects where an incredibly heightened sense of perception. At the time after my return from Arizona, I was working at a corner store. With every customer that came in the store I could see three people. I could see who they were as a physical human being standing in front of me. I could see what all there issues were internally and I could see who they were as a higher soul. It got to the point that working there was impossible because I thought I would lose my sanity. So I took some time off to just be, and to try and find a way back to live within the human population. But it did not come easy.

Trying to be human is a very interesting thing. You go through a process that will inevitably reveal what you believe being human is. For me that was returning to the only consistent thing I had ever known in my life, various forms of addiction. For me, to be human was to hide from myself. Whether the addiction was men, books, food, work, talking or sleeping, I would completely absorb myself in one at a time, while I was trying to find a way to feel human again. I was trying to find a way to feel comfortable around other people while in a highly sensitized state. It took a very long time before I would be able run far enough from who I was, that I ran back into myself. It has been 20 years in fact, since most of these events took place. There have been many relationships, many diets, many many books and many miles spent looking for who I am and where I belong. After all of this I have come to a very simple decision. I don't belong.

Perhaps an explanation is due at this time. Most of my years growing up, I never felt like I belonged. Life obliged me with the opportunity on many occasions to prove this true. I always felt like I was an outsider. All through school I never really even tried to fit in, people never seemed to be my tribe. As I got older and became an adult, I gravitated to what was unusual, spirituality, the occult any unusual understanding of reality. The thing that set me apart is where I felt comfortable but it was a lonely existence. I denied with every breath that I wasn't happy, because I had convinced myself that I was. However there was always something missing. In truth there has been something missing since the day I was born. For me the missing part was what most people understood to be the unseen world. The reality that lived beyond the veils. Without understanding it, I had come to live in two completely different worlds. One world I was comfortable in and it felt like home, where I was supposed to be, but for the most part I was the only one who lived there. Then there was the world that was commonly shared by all the people. I was very uncomfortable in this reality but the need to be around other beings that looked like me was undeniably strong. I was never able to form a sense of home or a sense of belonging. For a very short period of time I had found that concept in Arizona. I have been searching for it ever since. The sense of not belonging for me was all consuming. It was everywhere I went. I have lived in some very beautiful places but after a while, they start feeling empty. It is only now that I am starting to understand this condition.

We are all on a journey. The journey is personal and individual. We have our lessons to learn and love to find. However for some of us, because of the life we come into, we start looking in the wrong places from the beginning. I am as human as anyone else, but I have never felt human. I have never been able to relate to what it is to be human. Whether it is because I was not properly taught to be human as a child, or perhaps my close relationship with animals had an affect, I really don't know why I was like this. Perhaps I have been too self contained in my life. Perhaps I am just a dreamer and I do not want to identify with what I think human beings represent. Truth is, I will never know why I was the way I was. The other truth is, it doesn't matter. The process I have gone through in the last 3 years of my life has taught me, that for feeling so little human, I had become the most human of them all. I had become completely self contained in a reality that existed only in my mind. That is what it is to be human. I had become the very thing I thought I could not identify with.

All the years of what I perceived as "failed everything", had brought me to a point of being a crumbled mess. I was that blob on the floor laying there crying out to the Universe, "Why me?. What did I do to deserve this? I am not a bad person, am I? If I hadn't done this, or If I had only done that" Throw in a bunch of, "I should have's" and that was pretty much where I was at. I had come full circle, I was where I was 20 years ago, swimming in a sea of self pity. Well no, to be honest I wasn't swimming, I was drowning. A part of me really wanted to die, but I would not abandon my dogs. They didn't deserve to pay for my idiocy.

So after 18 months or so of projecting a confident, capable, happy person to the world around me but literally dying inside from despair, I had my moment. I remember to this day with crystal clarity. I was laying on my bed, a dog on either side of me, almost asleep and it floated in very calmly and quietly. I had no idea who I was. As this understanding grew and formed in my mind I realized I had become nothing more than an echo of everyone else's desires. I was not living in my life. My life had become an attempt to be what people had wanted me to be since I was a child. I had no identity, human or otherwise. This understanding hit me like a sledge hammer right between the eyes.

How could I have missed this? It really overwhelmed me as so many memories came flooding back into my mind, hearing the voices telling me what I was or who I should be. Not that they were hurtful or painful memories, most were memories of lovely people telling me I should write or teach, maybe I need to work with animals, I need to be a counsellor. Over and over, it was a constant stream of other people's voices creating my future. I have heard a lot of people talk about the dreams they have, the goals that are important to them. I have never felt that. I am a very passionate person but to have a specific dream for the future to work towards and put all my energy into? That has never been an experience I have had. The truth is I have never been driven towards a future of any kind. Now I knew why, all the future's that have been in my head, what I thought I should be working towards, were never my vision for myself.

So what do you do when you have that realization? In truth I wasn't sure. Sure I know the basics, start to figure out what it is you genuinely like and climb the ladder from there. I knew the how to version, but for me, I needed more. I knew I had to go right back to the very first memories I had. I also knew I had to discover my natural leanings. I needed to know if what I thought was natural, actually was or was it implanted in me so early that I just came to think of it as natural. In those few moments my life had started anew. I had no idea it would take me on a path with such varied topography. The path has not been straight nor has it been easy. However the path has brought me to who it is that I Am.

There were many voices that had been in my head telling me who I was that were very difficult to release. Some of those voices had been there for 30 years. I came to realize some of the voices were very appealing to me because of the image they represented. Some voices were appealing because they served my need for acknowledgement. In truth I honour each voice that was there, because in the moment I heard that voice, it served a greater need in me to fill part of my void. And this brings me to what this whole book has been about. This book I have written in the guise of offering others the understanding that much of what they may feel or experience is still true even though they may not be able to physically prove it, however in truth this book has been my journey home.

It is the void in all of us that connects us. If we all came here as completely whole people there would be nothing to share. It is the fact that we have holes all through ourselves that connect us to other people, so they can help us fill the holes. It is our connection to others that allow us to be human, it allows us to understand the power of vulnerability. And through the power of vulnerability we can grow beyond human, and become humanity. I was very fortunate to have the crazy, painful, topsy turvy life I have had, it was a blessing. Without it I am not sure I would be here today with you, able to feel you, through me.

My journey home has been the journey to myself, to understand the difference between connecting with others, and adopting the desires that they project upon you. As children it is so important that we develop a solid sense of self, but we can only do that if we allow the holes within us to be filled with experiences that provide us with the opportunity to decide for ourselves what we hear echoing back to us. I think all of us have a certain degree of adopted opinions, that have shaped our lives. That is not always a bad thing. Sometimes someones opinion is very valuable in helping you shape your own. Seeing things from all angles and exploring new areas bring variety to life. However knowing the difference between what belongs to you and what belongs to others is vital for any kind of self identity.

We come into this world with holes. Those holes are meant to be filled with experiences and emotion, teaching and understanding, and in some cases they are. It is how we learn to be human, to identify in some way with the society that surrounds us. Far too often though those holes do not get filled in a way that allows us to feel intact. In many cases the holes remain empty and when we are older we try to fill them with stuff. Stuff often makes us feel less empty temporarily, but then we need to put more and more stuff in our holes because stuff never really fills them how they need to be filled. When the holes do not get filled as a child we always have a sense of abandonment. We are empty, parts of us are missing and we are not taught how to fill them. As we get older this graduates to self abandonment. We live our lives doing what we are told to do, or doing what we think is the right thing, but never being able to connect to ourselves in the doing of it. Whenever we connect to what we think is our lives, we are in fact connecting to the life someone else said we should live.

I think this problem is epidemic in our society. It is so easy to abandon yourself. Most people do not totally abandon themselves, they make just enough of their own decisions to allow themselves to think they are living their own lives. But they still feel hollow. This is the worst kind of abandonment, it is the hardest to discover. The life where everything appears to of your making, but you still can't connect to it, and if you cannot connect to it, you can't own it. You will not be responsible for something you do not own.

That inability to connect to your life leads to the sense of separation and that leads to abandonment. It is my opinion that this process is the basis for ninety nine percent of substance abuse, and to go out there on a limb, I also think it plays a role in the development of Dementia and Alzheimers. In the bigger picture abandonment is visible everywhere at all times. We have abandoned the very planet we live on. We have abandoned our elderly, our children our health care systems. We live in a cesspool of abandonment and we are all drowning. So what does it take to fill up our holes? It really just takes one thing, connection through positive reflection.

What does that mean? It is simple. We all need to fill our holes with who we truly are. That can only happen if it is being reflected back to us in a positive light. We need to feel the connection to another as a stream of energy, not as a group of words that label who we are supposed to be. We need to be as aware of what we are projecting as we are of what we are receiving. Ask yourself a question. When you experience someone you think has a special talent, how long does it take your mind to start thinking about what it is they should be doing? A few seconds, perhaps? Almost immediately you are thinking to yourself, "Wow, that guy should be on TV, or that girl really needs to be on stage" Now may I ask ever so politely, "How the hell do you know what they need?" There that wasn't so bad, was it?

What I am saying is none of us know the path that anyone is on. In truth we do not know why someone has the talent they have. All we should know is that this person has crossed our path for a reason. We should then start digging into our own life to see what that reason is. It is entirely possible they have crossed our path for some encouragement on theirs. However, maybe they crossed our path to show us, we need to be willing to put our own talents out there. Perhaps they came into our life so we could just experience a moment of profound beauty. We may never know why they are there, maybe it doesn't matter. All I know for sure is that telling anyone what it is they should do is a double edge sword. If someone asks your opinion, sometimes the smartest thing to do is to return a questions with a question. Something like this, "What is it you would like to do with your talent?" This encourages the person to explore their own desires, and fill their own holes.

This is also the process to filling your own holes. My journey back to myself came down to three questions, "Is this true for me? Is this what I feel? Is this what I need?" It was a long process and it took a few years. In all truth I am quite sure the journey may never be totally over. I do know though, that my understanding of who I am and where I am going has changed drastically in the last 18 months. I am walking a path that is completely unfamiliar to me, but it feels incredible. A couple of the voices that I had held on to so long were do deeply integrated in me that when I released them I had physical reactions. For a few minutes to a few hours there was tremendous insecurity and a sense of grasping for something, anything that could fill the vacancy I had just created. I had a panicked feeling that I had no identity again. If I let go of this, the entire structure of my reality would come tumbling down. In truth some of that did happen. A huge part of my being felt tremendous guilt about abandoning someone else's dream for me. It wasn't a bad dream it was just the wrong dream. I struggled with the guilt and the knowing that even after I had let go of that voice, the voice would continue to echo in my life.

Those voices are the hardest to let go of. The ones that in and of themselves are lovely dreams carried by the voices of people that care for you, and they are not ready to understand, that they are projecting the needs of their own lives on to you. They truly do not understand the damage they are doing by dreaming a beautiful life for you. The only problem is, it is not the dream you want for yourself, it is an empty dream. What compounds the problem is that for many years you may have participated in the dream, when you kept trying to make it your dream. What I came to understand through all this was that I was abandoning myself and replacing my voice with someone else's, but what I didn't realize initially was that by doing this, I was also indulging the other person's voice in abandoning themselves. I was helping them to deny the need of that dream for themselves, under the illusion that the dream was about me. By adopting their dream in my life, it allowed them to not be responsible for their own dream. And that is how abandonment becomes a raging plague throughout society.

It is a vicious cycle that can only be stopped by standing still and detaching from all the voices in your life that are not your own. It is in this way that you can actually hear what your voice sounds like, without the voices of all the well wishers. Once you hear your own voice, you can allow it to become the guiding light to sculpt your life. Please do not allow this to turn into the blame game. You are as responsible for adopting someone else's voice as they are for projecting it on you. Blame has never solved anything and it never will.

This is the lesson the Alien really sought to teach me. It is the lesson most of us on the planet need to learn. It took me 20 years to hear this simple truth. I hope you are wiser than me. Just because we have no longer chosen to follow a path that leads us to the Grey's does not mean that we haven't abandoned our future in other ways. I think everyone reading this right now could think of many ways abandonment affect their own lives. What affects us personally, ripples out into society. We have abandoned Mother Earth to the point that we are in the process of abandoning her literally. Abandoning this Earth is merely a reflection of how we have abandoned ourselves. As I write this, plans are going forward to colonize Mars. How is it that we will treat Mars any better than Earth if we have not learned to stop abandoning ourselves. In truth it is a most profound reflection that we are abandoning a planet so rich and full of variety for a dead planet. We cannot fill our own holes, so we fill the earth full of stuff. We abandon ourselves because we cannot see the incredible beauty we are, and we replace it with something that is hollow and lifeless, because this better represents the holes that we feel inside. The spaces we do not know how to fill up. If we are to change this, we need to connect on a healthy positive level. To see what we are doing, we have to stop being blind to our own needs. Just start by asking yourself one simple question, What makes you happy? Your life is an empty canvas. It is not only your right, it is your obligation, to paint something beautiful. Paint who you are inside, that part of yourself that is so afraid to be seen lest you be destroyed. It is in that part of you that you will hear your own voice. It is in that part of you that you will find your truth.

My journey has been an incredible one. The power in this journey however is not the Alien interaction, it is the human story. It is my greatest hope that all of you will love yourself enough to connect to the Alien within you, so that in that grey dark place you can find the human that you are. If we all find our human, perhaps there is still hope for us to join together in our humanity. Within that, lies the power, to fill up our holes.

Acknowledgements

I really want to acknowledge all the people that were part of this journey. Many of them are no longer here in this vibration. Many that I was close to, our paths have gone in different directions. Many I am still fortunate to know. Though it is not possible to thank every person individually, there are a few I would like to give special mention to:

Marilyn Picard

Lynette Brooker

Kathie Groomes

Olinda Fernandes

All my Exes for all the lessons

All of my Family

My Family from the Blue Millennium, wherever they are!

But most of all, I must thank my dogs for their patience, their love and their marvellous bladders when I was in the zone!

Thank you so much for reading this book.

Please feel free to contact me for book signings or lectures. You can also contact me about any of my other services

Website:

www.rosemcmullen.com

Facebook:

https://www.facebook.com/rose.mcmullen.33

May you all be blessed with peace and joy

www.ingramcontent.com/pod-product-compliance
Lightning Source LLC
Chambersburg PA
CBHW071539040426
42452CB00008B/1067